INSPIRED CORRESPONDENCES TO THE RIGHTEOUS

Living LETTERS

AN ANTHOLOGY

FOUNDING AUTHOR
PSALMIST RAINE

LIVING LETTERS
Inspired Correspondences to the Righteous

Founding Author:
Psalmist Raine
therefreshteam@berefresh.com

Contributing Authors:
Lisa Michelle Beeler
Elisha Davis
Earlye Julien
Allana Lewis
Alissia Miles
Lizbeth Pioquinto
Joy Smith
Tonthalell Walters

ISBN: 978-1-943343-27-0
Printed in the USA.

Published by:
Destined To Publish | Flossmoor, Illinois
www.DestinedToPublish.com

Table of Contents

INTRODUCTION

THE URGENCY

To the enduring believers of faith in this present time, I bid you great grace and peace in the name of our Lord and Savior Jesus Christ. I come to present some words of encouragement and edification to you as you press through the times of your living. I do this not of my own ambition, but by the leading of the One who is Sovereign and Holy; by the authority of our Righteous Reigning King, Christ Jesus our Lord; and by the Sweet Communion of the Holy Spirit. This is the time, now more than ever, for us to move with God, the one known as Elohim. For as you know, there are many gods on Earth.

There are many deities that even the very elect are bowing to. It is the perfect time—the set time to be girded up in our call and sure of our election in Christ Jesus. As you know, and as it has been proclaimed in the Holy Scriptures, our adversary is like a roaring lion seeking whom he may devour (1 Peter 5:8). He has been on the prowl for quite some time. He seeks to cause internal conflict and makes bold attempts to convince the sons of God to reverse their allegiance. He has been able to deceive many with their love for a truth that is rooted in logic and carnality; but this has not been the truth that comes from the Lord.

We have seen many believers confused by the various voices and opinions pouring out in this present time. It has created instability in our faith. Some of these opinions come from the voices of those who think they are masterminds and experts. These "masterminds" have demonstrated sensitivity to spiritual matters but have failed to submit to the Lordship of Jesus Christ. This approach to spiritual matters breeds confusion in the masses, and as we can see, it is growing exponentially. This is the hour that the Lord wants to gird you up with intel and revelation that will fuel your press.

As you engage in reading, I would like for you to consider the weight of this work. This correspondence was birthed as a tool for you to be reminded to hold fast to the truth that we all have once read throughout the pages of the Holy Scriptures. We have stored some of these treasures in our hearts as we have vowed that we would not sin against God (Psalms 119:11). This correspondence is a way that God has designed to keep you equipped in the battle. Every word you read, we pray that it will spark a remembrance of the promises of God to the uncompromising righteous ones. As your sister in the Lord, I encourage you to keep standing. We need each other.

The generations coming behind you, the cloud of witnesses that have gone before you, are rooting for you to stand. Those that have been martyred in this world took a stance as an example of righteousness to you. We know by the revelation of the Lord Jesus that these are the times when our light has to shine and shine brightly, more now than ever before. These are the times when we are entrusted with preserving the way of the Lord. For His way is true, right, and just. His way considers eternal factors and weights concealed for an appointed time.

We cannot afford to let the Lord's name go in vain. Not on our watch! He has triumphed over our enemies, breaking the power of wickedness off of our lives. Today, you are standing as a testament of His Power and Grace. You are living as a strong witness of our true and reigning King. The truth of the matter is that beyond the scope of flesh and blood, your existence and your obedience are a witness today to those in the Heavenlies of the power and wisdom of our God (Ephesians 3:10). It makes my heart glad to know that there are more who are enduring the tests and trials of faith. I want to remind you that you are not alone.

The purpose of this correspondence is that the Lord has you on His mind as you endure the fiery tests that come your way. Recall the way our Lord handled the suggestions of lawlessness and deception with the enemy. You need to remember how the Lord gave the children of Israel strategy for battle. You need to remember the effects that take place when we lay down our stance. Our stance in our obedience to the word of the Lord is doing more than anyone can articulate. It is making a mark on Earth greater than we can perceive right now. Many will watch, study, and hear about those who righteously stood for the Lord. May this be the tool that fulfills its call to encourage you. May it give you exactly what you need as you journey through your time.

Jesus prayed this prayer: *"I do not pray that You should take them out of the world, but that You should keep them from the evil one"* (John 17:15 NKJV). This is the time, more now than ever, that we hold on to the help of the Lord to sustain us while we stand representing the Kingdom of our

God. This is the time. Endure—knowing that the reward is just on the other side.

With this great thought in mind and as a fellow laborer in this work, let us press toward the mark that is in Christ Jesus our Lord. Let us bring great delight to our Father by standing for Him in perilous and peaceful times. Let the light of His glory shine brightly for all the world to see through you. May you arise as the salt of the earth, preserving territories, regions, and nations for His Glory. It is all possible through Jesus Christ our Lord. Outside of Him, you will not be able to accomplish this righteous work.

Sincerely, I am convinced that we will see the power of the Lord's might and love through you. I know He has called you for this marked time in His Glory.

Father, in Jesus' name alone, I ask that you keep your precious ones as they stand in the splendor of your glory, shining brightly on Earth for you. May those who see Your light draw nigh to Your Glory and see their salvation. May the darkness of iniquity, rebellion, and pride be completely extinguished from the shine of Your glorious light. May the sons of righteousness, those known as the heritage of God, live as strong witnesses of Your might and power both now and forevermore. Amen!

ELISHA DAVIS

DECLARING THE RIGHTFUL KING

WORSHIP THAT ENTHRONES THE KING, DETHRONES THE ENEMY, AND BRINGS ORDER

Do you ever feel like your worship has no power or meaning? Do you ever feel like heaven doesn't hear you? Allow this letter to encourage you; your worship is the invitation God is looking for to set Himself as King in your life. His reign in your life will change you and everything around you for eternity.

Who sits on the throne of our lives? This isn't a rhetorical question. Let's take a moment to really think about who sits on the highest seat of our lives. We have to identify this to determine what or with whom we have come into alignment. We cannot be ignorant in this regard. The one who is enthroned rules, judges, and frames our reality. I can remember a season of my life when I allowed everything and anything to occupy the throne of my life. My heart was full of anxiety, fear, depression, and constant worry. All of these occupied the highest position in my life while I served in church on a regular basis. You might ask, "How is that possible if you're in church?" It was actually quite easy; I did nothing at all. I did not spend time communing with the Father. I only prayed and fasted when I wanted something, and I served to feel like I was a "good Christian." I naturally have a quiet demeanor, so not many people noticed the chaos brewing inside because of the strongholds that reigned on the throne of my life. But I knew there was complete disorder.

It's interesting how doing nothing at all can lead to such unrest, disorder, and turmoil. I'm reminded of the story in 1 Kings 1, where King David was on his deathbed, and his son, Adonijah, decided to take over the throne. Initially, David didn't do anything to stop Adonijah, and soon after, things fell out of order. Solomon's mother, Bathsheba, and David's advisors had to remind David that Solomon was the rightful heir to the throne. Similarly, I had to be reminded of who should occupy the throne of my heart. At the time, I was taking a ministry class on healing and deliverance, and the teacher stated, "There's no healing or deliverance outside of God's Word." Then the teacher changed my life. He said, "If you're not reading the Word daily and spending time with God, then you cannot continue this class." I knew I needed healing and deliverance because I was dealing with the chaos in my heart. So, I committed to spending time with the Father by reading the Word every single day. And guess what?! I started hearing the LORD. He began speaking to me about unforgiveness, anger, fear, trauma, and all the other usurpers that had taken a seat on the throne of my heart. The more time I spent reading and praying, the more I understood the person and character of the Father. As I understood His person and character, my faith grew, and I was able to trust Him to sit on the throne of my heart. I was walking in healing and freedom for the first time in a long time. I didn't realize the LORD, in all His goodness, was setting me up. The Father was teaching me how to worship Him in spirit and in truth. This worship prepared me for the most challenging test of my life ... cancer.

After consistently spending time with the LORD, I found myself excited to hear what He would say every morning through His Word. Being with Him was, and is, amazing. Peace and order filled my days. Then one day, I felt a lump. After several tests, I was diagnosed with breast cancer. And here's what worshipping in spirit and truth did: It maintained the peace and order established by the King! Elohim the Creator, Jehovah Shalom, Jehovah Rapha had been seated on the throne of my life, and He wasn't stirred by a cancer diagnosis; therefore, I wasn't stirred. I remember a mother of the church asking me how I was feeling after the diagnosis. I told her I was at peace and believed Jehovah Rapha would heal me. She asked me how I could be so sure, and I said the first thing that came to mind. I told her that since God had proven Himself to be faithful as the Healer of my heart, I trusted Him to be faithful as the Healer of my body. This was the setup! In drawing closer to the Father and learning how to worship Him with my life (not just through singing during church service), trusting Him became my knee-jerk response. I thought all those mornings in devotion were just about deliverance from some past issues. I didn't realize the LORD was healing my past and preparing me to receive healing in my future.

My response to the church mother showed how God's order was established in me because I gave Him the throne. You see, we don't have to focus on dethroning the enemy. We only need to commit to enthroning the rightful King through a lifestyle of worship. If you go back to the story in 1 Kings 1, when David finally declared Solomon as king, all things began to fall into place. Adonijah immediately stopped his attempt to usurp the throne. Your commitment and devotion to worshipping the LORD God will cause the enemy to abandon the throne of your heart. There is no principality, power, or ruler that can withstand the I AM.

Now, understand that just because the enemy abandons the throne doesn't mean he won't attempt to hold on to things in your life. In 1 Kings, when Adonijah abandoned the throne, he ran and took hold of the horns of the altar to avoid being killed by Solomon. The enemy will try this in your life even when you've committed to being a worshipper of the Most High. He will go as far as looking for anything in close proximity to you so he can hold on and try to find a new foothold. As I underwent cancer treatment, I saw where the enemy would use people's responses to the diagnosis to try and cast doubt and fear within me. People gave false prophesies and even claimed that my husband and I needed their specific prayers in order to see my healing. The biggest attempt to get me back in a place of fear, anxiety, unrest, and chaos came the day after I finished my final radiation treatment: I received news that my mother had died. I literally heard the enemy taunt me and ask if I would still worship. He didn't ask about anything else. He was only concerned with the position I would give God in my life. This was his opportunity.

You know what I did? Although physically very weak from treatments, I got up, walked just outside the door of our apartment, and worshipped the Father. That's right, on the day my mom died, I worshipped. It wasn't long and drawn out. It was extremely difficult, but through my worship, I was determined to declare that there was only one King, and I would worship Him no matter what. That decision silenced the enemy ... literally. There were no more horns of the altar for him to grab hold of. Worship is powerful!

Enthroning the Righteous One in our worship sets our world in order without fail. Dethroning the enemy is a byproduct of genuine worship. Dethroning might sound very spiritual, but it's not. To dethrone is to simply "remove or drive from a throne; to divest of rule or power" (Webster's Dictionary 1828). We've been given free will to choose who we want to remove from the throne and who we want to sit on the throne of our hearts. The enemy doesn't have a right to the throne unless you agree with him. Remember I said that I struggled with all kinds of issues. It was because I agreed with the enemy through my inaction. My inaction left the throne wide open for the enemy to take a seat. When I decided to declare the LORD God Almighty as King by devoting my time and making a commitment to Him, I divested the enemy of his rule and power over my life. The only way to bring order in your world is to dethrone the enemy by worshipping and enthroning the One True Living God.

Enthroning the LORD through our worship is done by honoring Him with love and extreme submission (Webster's Dictionary 1828). Love and submission require our ALL. Our love and submission are natural responses to the revelation of a glorious and holy Creator. To submit means to yield, to put in subjection, to obey ... but not begrudgingly ... instead, with "a voluntary attitude of giving in, cooperating, and carrying a burden" (Blue Letter Bible, G5283). Submitting to God never stops. As I was going through treatment, I constantly had to check my heart posture because it was so easy to complain, be frustrated, and be scared.

One day, my worship required that I submit to and declare this truth, "If I live, I live. If I die, I die. God is good." The truth of who God was wasn't predicated on my outcome. This was my intentional attitude of giving in. I wasn't giving in to death but giving in to the truth that He is glorious, righteous, holy, all powerful, and awesome because He is Jehovah. My worship doesn't need to be attached to what He's done for me. It's established in all the facets of His being that I can comprehend. (John 4:23-24 NKJV) states that *"... the true worshippers will worship the Father in spirit and truth ..."* We have to ask ourselves if we can worship the rightful King regardless of the outcome. True worship has its foundation in the truth of who God is. In Exodus 3:13-15, God reveals His name to Moses at the burning bush. He tells Moses *"I AM THAT I AM."* In Hebrew, the name is Haya Asher Haya. The word *asher* means "that, which, what, who, when, how, because." The LORD God revealed to Moses that He exists as the "that," the "who," the "which," the "what," the "how," the "because," and the "when" (Blue Letter Bible App). Since He is all things, all thrones belong to Him. Our worship is rooted in this. The deeper we go into the Word of God, the more revelation we receive about the person and character of God. The more revelation we receive about the personality of the LORD, the more we are expected to submit, devote, and pour ourselves out to Him. We are also expected to declare His name in every circumstance. The acts of submission, devotion, pouring out, and declaration *are* worship.

Consider the throne of your heart. Who or what sits on that seat in your life? Is there anything attempting to hold on to the horns of the altar in your life? Have you been inactive and left a vacancy for the enemy to take up the throne? Have you made a commitment to commune with the LORD? You get to make the decision about who you want on the throne. There is One Rightful King, and He requires you to make that declaration through a lifestyle of worship. Our submission and surrender in worship mean we are giving the LORD free reign in our world. This reign has led to my healing, deliverance, peace, and the most beautiful thing of all ... drawing closer to the Father. Once you give the Eternal King free reign, every usurper flees, and God's judgments, laws, and precepts bring order to your life. God is awaiting the invitation of your worship. Will you commit to worship that enthrones the Rightful King in every area of your life today?

Elisha Davis

....

Elisha Davis is a wife, proud mother of two, and breast cancer survivor. She is a devoted intercessor at Worship Life Church in Goodyear, AZ, and writes from a place of deep faith and love for the Lord. She hopes to inspire others to continually dedicate themselves to the Lord.

Allana Lewis

Seeking Divine Alignment, Finding the Heart of God

To the believer in Jesus Christ who desires to grow deeper in their love and fellowship with God:

Have you ever misplaced something valuable to you? You go on a search for what's missing, and while in pursuit of what you misplaced, you find an entirely different item—something of importance that you were not intentionally looking for at the time. This scenario happens to me often. Perhaps you are one of those highly organized people who always knows exactly where everything is. But if you are like me, there is a good chance you can relate to the experience of finding a surprise while in the midst of looking for something else. You may be able to relate to another example.

Have you ever discovered the lyrics to a song you've been singing for years aren't actually correct? When I was younger, there was a popular television show called *Good Times*. Its catchy theme song would play at the start of every episode, and I would sing along. Years later, I was surprised to learn that the lyrics I had been singing were way off from the actual words. An internet search led to the revelation of the true song content, and, sadly, the lyrics were not about "good times"—it was quite the opposite.

I remember laughing in surprise when discovering my mistake. This experience also made me wonder—how often do we assume we know something only to later realize we were wrong? This may be the case in our relationship with the Lord. If we do not actively seek God's heart, we may unknowingly be holding onto beliefs or traditions that don't align with His word.

Encountering new information that shifts our understanding can play a major part in our journey of growing in God. Sometimes these discoveries come as pleasant surprises, but other times, they can be deeply unsettling. As we grow in our relationship with God, we learn more about His ways and uncover more insight into what is in His heart. In Isaiah 55:8-9 (ESV), the Lord declares, *"For My thoughts are not your thoughts, neither are your ways My ways, declares the Lord. For as the heavens are higher than the earth, so are My ways higher than your ways, and My thoughts than your thoughts."*

Just as we sometimes stumble upon new discoveries in everyday life—whether it's finding an item we weren't looking for or realizing we've misheard lyrics—our spiritual journey often leads to revelations that challenge what we once believed. This is exactly what happened to King Josiah when he uncovered God's law. His discovery led to a profound transformation. Responding well when learning the truth of God's ways and thoughts makes all the difference in our relationship with Him.

The story of King Josiah provides a powerful example of what it looks like to humbly respond when discovering that an aspect of our life is out of alignment with God's will. Josiah uncovered something he was not searching for, but the knowledge he gained deeply impacted him, his family lineage, and his entire nation. Beyond something as simple as the mere lyrics to a song, he discovered that the entire system of worship within his nation was offensive to God.

According to 2 Kings 22, Josiah became king of Jerusalem at the early age of eight years old. Even as a young king, he earnestly sought to do what was right in the sight of the Lord, modeling his leadership after the righteous forefathers of his lineage. After eighteen years of leadership, King Josiah found out some mind-blowing information. He discovered something that completely shattered his understanding of what he thought was right in his relationship with God.

In the process of restoring the temple, King Josiah's administration discovered the Book of the Law. It was as though someone had uncovered the true "lyrics" of a song Josiah had been singing, only to reveal that the tune he thought was beautiful was offensive to God. The written word of God showed Josiah how the nation's entire system of worship was corrupt. The people of Jerusalem, including King Josiah's own ancestors, had been operating in disobedience to God's laws for generations. In modern day vernacular, he may have even said he "was today's years old" when he found out his forefathers' actions were not in alignment with God's word.

What a heartbreaking revelation! Can you imagine doing something for nearly two decades, believing it was right and acceptable in the eyes of the Lord, only to discover it was an open door to destruction? How could his forefathers allow this for so many generations? Well, leaders are not infallible. Proverbs 14:12 (ESV) warns us, *"There is a way that seems right to a man, but its end is the way of death."*

King Josiah was deeply grieved when he realized how far the nation had strayed from God's commands. Instead of ignoring this revelation or assuming he already knew the truth, Josiah sought God's wisdom. He didn't rely on tradition or personal understanding; he inquired of the Lord to determine the right course of action. This is the kind of intentional seeking God calls us to today.

King Josiah was bold and courageous, and his response was not random; it was a divine assignment. Long before Josiah's birth, God spoke through a prophet in 1 Kings 13:2, foretelling that a descendant of David named Josiah would rise to confront the corrupt system of worship in Jerusalem. Josiah was born to fulfill this purpose, just as we were each created to complete specific assignments God has prepared for us. As Ephesians 2:10 (NKJV) reminds us, *"For we are His workmanship, created in Christ Jesus for good works, which God prepared beforehand that we should walk in them."*

But Josiah's assignment was not easy. He had to come against a longstanding way of life in his family lineage. Generations before him, King Solomon, Josiah's ancestor, was instrumental in the establishment of worship in Jerusalem. Solomon contributed significantly to the level of defilement and idolatry present in the land. Though King Solomon had built and dedicated an immaculate temple to the Lord, his heart was eventually turned away from God by the foreign women he chose to love, who worshipped other gods. In 1 Kings 11, we read how King Solomon ignored warnings from the Lord and established several altars for the worship of false gods, leading the nation into widespread idolatry. This act of disobedience planted seeds of compromise that continued for generations, contributing to idolatry within the culture and normalizing the worship of false gods in Jerusalem.

In this instance, the enemy succeeded at craftily deceiving God's people. In Deuteronomy 32:16-17 (AMPC) God expresses His feelings toward idolatry: *"They provoked Him to jealousy with strange gods; with abominations they provoked Him to anger. They sacrificed to demons, not to God, to gods they had not known, to new gods that had come recently, whom your fathers did not fear."* The enemy was able to get God's people to fall down and worship him, an offer that Jesus was able to successfully refuse. We must continue to be on guard to ensure we are not deceived into a false system of worship.

When Josiah learned the truth, he acted. He courageously decided to break the cycle of disobedience to God. He did not allow fear of breaking from cultural norms or family traditions to hinder him. Instead, he destroyed the altars to false gods, removed the idols from the temple, and led the nation in renewing their covenant with the Lord. Josiah's reforms brought true Godly worship back to the land and restored what had been defiled.

King Josiah's response is a powerful reminder for us today. While we are no longer under the Old Testament law, Jesus came to fulfill the law and bring us into a new covenant. Yet, as we grow in our knowledge of God's ways, we may discover areas in our lives that are out of alignment with His word, especially if we are seeking to love the Lord with all our heart, soul, mind, and strength. It takes effort on our part to learn of God's ways and to love the way He desires to be loved. As He stated in John 14:15 (NKJV), *"If you love Me, keep My commandments."* John 15:12-14 (NKJV) states, *"This is my commandment, that you love one another as I have loved you. Greater love has no one than this, than to lay down one's life for his friends. You are My friends if you do whatever I command you."* The scriptures let us know that obedience to His word is an expression of our love to God.

It is not enough to assume that our ways of living are pleasing to God simply because they are popular in society. Proverbs 3:5-6 (NKJV) reminds us, *"Trust in the Lord with all your heart, and lean not on your own understanding; in all your ways acknowledge Him, and He shall direct your paths."*

How can we ensure that our lives are pleasing to the Lord? First, we must study His word. 2 Timothy 2:15 (KJV) urges us to *"study to show yourself approved unto God, a workman that needeth not to be ashamed, rightly dividing the word of truth."* In addition to studying, we also should seek God's guidance through prayer. Matthew 7:7-8 (NKJV) assures us, *"Ask, and it will be given to you; seek, and you will find; knock, and it will be opened to you."* God is faithful to reveal His heart to those who diligently seek Him.

As we grow in our relationship with God, we must allow the Holy Spirit to guide us into His truth. John 16:13-14 (NKJV) promises, *"However, when He, the Spirit of truth, has come, He will guide you into all truth; for He will not speak on His own authority, but whatever He hears He will speak; and He will tell you things to come. He will glorify Me, for He will take of what is Mine and declare it to you."*

Life may be filled with unexpected discoveries. Whether it's stumbling upon lost items, uncovering the real lyrics to a song, or—like King Josiah—learning that long-held beliefs or traditions do not align with God's truth, these revelations have the power to transform us. The real question is: *How will we respond?*

Josiah's response teaches us that when we are confronted with truth, we must seek God's heart rather than holding onto our own understanding. True alignment with Him requires humility, surrender, and a willingness to let go of what feels familiar or comfortable in order to embrace what is right in God's eyes.

But this alignment doesn't happen passively. Just as Josiah pursued God's will and took bold action, we too must actively seek God's heart. Asking God to reveal areas where we need transformation, studying His word to understand His ways, and being sensitive to His voice in prayer leads to deeper fellowship with God. Being open to correction, having a willingness to change course, and being committed to loving God in the way He desires to be loved help to bring us into divine alignment.

Jesus Himself set the ultimate example when He said, *"Not My will, but Yours, be done"* (Luke 22:42 NKJV). He showed us that true love for God is not just about words or traditions—it is about obedience, devotion, and a heart fully surrendered to Him.

When seeking God's heart and divine alignment, invite the Holy Spirit to reveal areas that need adjustments. Take time to reflect on the ways He is leading you into greater purpose, freedom, and blessings. Here are some example questions to spark your discoveries:

- *Are my actions and decisions truly aligned with God's will?* Am I stewarding my finances and responsibilities in a way that honors Him?
- *How do I treat those closest to me?* Are my relationships—whether with my spouse, children, or friends—reflecting God's love, grace, and truth? Do I need to make adjustments within these relationships in a way that honors Him?
- *Are there cultural or family traditions I have embraced that God is calling me to let go of?* On the other hand, are there godly values and traditions I can preserve and pass down to future generations?

- *Could I be the one chosen to shift the spiritual direction of my family?* How might God be calling me to break negative cycles and establish a new legacy of faith, obedience, and blessing?
- *Is there something I participate in that "seems right" but is not actually aligned with God's heart? How can I replace anything displeasing to God with habits and commitments that bring me closer to Him?*
- *Are there affiliations, partnerships, or organizations I am connected to that are not pleasing to God?* Do I need to reassess the things I align myself with?
- *Has God called me to confront a corrupt system—whether in my family, workplace, or nation?* If so, how can I step into that role with both boldness and wisdom, knowing that He has equipped me for the task?

Remember, God does not expose areas of misalignment to condemn, but because of His love, He draws us closer to His heart, His truth, and His best for our lives. God is always ready to reveal more of Himself to those who seek Him. May we take time to be still and hear what His Spirit has to reveal to us. Here is a prayer to assist you as you seek:

"Father, I thank you for being the revealer of all truth. Your word is a lamp unto my feet and a light to my path. Guide every decision I make with Your spirit of wisdom. I humble myself and ask You to expose any hidden areas in my life that are not pleasing to You. Come against any area where I may be deceived, and open my eyes of understanding. Forgive me for operating any area of my life in a way that is contrary to

Your word. Because I love You with all my heart and want to live in Your will, I ask that You remove all scales from my eyes. Because You are my strength and my shield, I can come out of agreement with all things that are not pleasing to You and move in boldness in the way You guide me. Your love for me is great. I will fulfill every plan You have for me. Be glorified in every area of my life. In the name of Jesus, I pray. Amen."

With love in Christ,

Allana

Allana Lewis is a native of Monroe, Louisiana. She serves as an adjunct associate professor and physician assistant in Atlanta, Georgia. She makes her writing debut with *Living Letters Anthology*. In addition to being passionate about holistic wellness, she enjoys traveling, cycling, music, and art.

Facebook and Instagram @ StandOnTheStone.

Tonthalell Walters

A Letter to the Ekklesia

I, Tonthalell, a bondservant of Yeshua and the Beloved of YHVH (Yahweh), a Son of the Faith and a Daughter of His Presence, write this letter to you with all sincerity and sobriety. My love for you runs deep and wide, as I long to see the expanse of your latter glory stretch across the earth, heralding the greatness, power, majesty, and dominion of our Father, Yahweh, and our Adoni, Yeshua HaMashiach.

Though His coming is imminent, and many saints are raptured/gathered daily, His return for the collective Body and His reign—establishing a new heaven and a new earth—is both nearer than times past and yet further than we can comprehend. Therefore, we must continue in the Faith and occupy until He returns in all His Splendor. As we await Him, we work while it is day, for the night comes ever so quickly (John 9:4).

The Bride is being adorned, purified, and set apart for the appearing of the Bridegroom (Revelation 19:7). Yet, in this present hour, many are being deceived and entangled with lesser loves, distracted by the world's appetites, driven by unsanctified ambitions, and directed by affections not anchored in Christ.

There are many things that we should focus our attention on while we wait, but I perceive these as some of the most important things to observe: Our Desires, Discipleship, and Devotion. These three pillars shape the very foundation of our walk with Yahweh. This Time is calling for *a people fashioned*, *forged*, and *formed* in the presence of the Almighty—vessels made fit for the Master's use and ready to manifest His Kingdom on earth.

FASHIONING HIS PEOPLE

Called to Holy Desire

Desire is the seat of the soul's direction. It is the inner compass that determines the course of a person's life. The Psalmist declares, *"Delight yourself also in the Lord, and He shall give you the desires of your heart"* (Psalm 37:4 NKJV). Yet, if our delights are unrefined, if our *appetites* are for what perishes, if our *ambitions* are self-driven, and if our *affections* are misplaced, our desires will lead us away from the narrow, ancient paths. The Lord is fashioning a people whose desires are sanctified, whose longings are set upon the things above (Colossians 3:1-2).

To be *fashioned* is to be shaped, molded, and refined according to the Divine pattern. This is the work of yielding to the potter's hand (Jeremiah 18:6). It is difficult for one to yield when the heart is in opposition. The clay resists the potter, insisting on its own way, as if it knows better how to serve the potter's purpose. Our priorities have fallen out of order, and we have lost our posture as yielded sons. When Yahweh begins to deal with a people's desires, He is initiating the process of fashioning them for a purpose far greater than one that is self-serving.

We have witnessed decades of moral failure, corruption, and spiritual neglect in the Body, all stemming from a man or woman's lack of holy desire. The world's fame, fortune, and power have bitten us, and, unlike David, we do envy the prosperity, wealth, success, and prominence of the wicked, and our foot has slipped (Psalm 73). *The current pulse and climate of the Body reveal that we have a desire issue: We no longer long for Him alone.*

The Word is clear: Those who chase after the things of the flesh are in opposition to those who pursue the things of the Spirit (Galatians 5:17). To be led by the Spirit is the mark of true sonship (Romans 8:14). The key to transforming our desires from unholy to holy lies in examining what drives our *appetites*, *ambitions*, and *affections*. What we hunger for, what we pursue, and what we love will reveal the true state of our desires.

Before Lot ended up in Sodom and Gomorrah, he first pitched his tent toward Sodom (Genesis 13:12). *His gaze shaped his appetite*. We have done the same in the Body today—turning our gaze toward the world and taking our eyes off Yeshua. It is no wonder we have compromised the sanctity of our places of worship; our gates have been feeding on the world's pleasures, and now they have become our desires—desires we have deceived ourselves into believing are normal or innate. We can no longer distinguish between sin and the Holy Spirit's desires. We have pitched our tents toward sin yet still expect sanctification.

We have found ourselves in a state of delusion. To be delivered from this great deception, we must sanctify our appetites. Fix your gaze back on the One who alone defines what is holy. He is sanctifying our appetites so that we may hunger and thirst for righteousness (Matthew 5:6).

Just as our appetites shape our desires, *our ambitions reveal the true motives of our hearts*. When ambition is left unsubmitted to Yahweh, it becomes a breeding ground for compromise, deception, and destruction. Judas Iscariot is a sobering example—his desire for power and position blinded him to the true riches found in Christ, leading him to betray the very One who could truly satisfy his soul. His unchecked ambition cost him his life. It didn't have to, but when personal gain, goals, and greed take precedence, one can end up sacrificing everything, only to gain death.

Many of us are like Judas: public friends of Yeshua yet private enemies, secretly conspiring with religious systems more concerned with controlling narratives and maintaining traditions than with empowering people to develop true intimacy with Abba.

Unchecked ambition corrupts our pursuits, but *misplaced affection warps our devotion*. What we love, we pursue, and what captures our hearts ultimately shapes our identity. If our affections are not anchored in Christ, they will be drawn toward things that gratify the flesh but starve the Spirit.

Misplaced and unchecked affections have the power to disqualify us from sonship. Scripture is clear: *those who are led by the Spirit are sons of God (Romans 8:14-15)*. If our affections are driven by the flesh, we forfeit our ability to walk in the Spirit. Our minds, hearts, and focus become consumed with pleasing the flesh, leaving no room for the refining work of sonship.

Many fail to take this truth seriously, which is why we see untamed affections manifesting in both pulpits and pews. We must confront what we love more than we love Love Himself. Adoni is sanctifying His people by refining our desires, dealing with our appetites, reshaping our affections, and purging our ambitions so that we are fully aligned with His will. This is the fashioning that prepares us for refinement to be priests of the Lord in today's world.

Prayer Point:

Lord, sanctify my desires. Refine my appetites, ambitions, and affections until they are wholly aligned with Your will and Your heart.

FORGING HIS PRIESTHOOD

THE REFINEMENT OF DISCIPLESHIP

To be *forged* is to be strengthened through fire, purified through pressure, and made resilient through resistance. It is the process of being tested and tempered for endurance. Discipleship is the crucible—the furnace where priests are fashioned, where a holy priesthood is prepared to minister before the Lord (1 Peter 2:9).

Aaron's priesthood was based on religious rituals, temporary appointments, and birthright succession. The Order of Melchizedek, by contrast, is founded on relationship, eternal establishment, and the calling and choosing of God. Because this original priesthood appears more relational than the structured Aaronic order, some have mistaken it for a life without discipleship. This is a grave error.

We cannot have an effective priesthood without discipleship. And true discipleship will bring discipline, establish new defaults, and shape us into distinct, holistic vessels fit for His service.

Discipline is not a bad word. In fact, the words "discipline" and "discipleship" both stem from the Latin *discipulus*, meaning "pupil" or "learner." Yet, in many ways, an *arrival mentality* has become the antagonist of our spiritual walk—a mindset that should not even be named among us. When we confront our unholy desires, appetites, ambitions, and affections, we recognize that the best posture is that of a lifelong learner—one who never *arrives* but instead *advances* as they become more conformed to the image of Christ.

We cannot develop disciples of Christ and disciples of *ourselves* at the same time. If we do, we fall into idolatry, turning those entrusted to us into *our* followers instead of leading them to Adoni. When we begin to discipline as though they are our sons and not His, we elevate ourselves as gods and make them our worshippers. Every act of discipline must flow from the love of the Father. We are merely stewards of His vineyard—either faithful or unfaithful. As priests, we hold a responsibility to the God we serve and to the people He entrusts to us. *We cannot build a solid kingdom of kings and priests while attempting to establish our own empire in the name of Yahweh.*

As mature sons and priests, we are refined beyond the weaknesses of our default nature. We no longer conform to the patterns of this world but are transformed by the renewing of our minds (Romans 12:2). We can no longer hide behind the excuses of "this is just how I am" or "I'm only human." To embrace such reasoning is to deny the power of transformation. It is to reject the very purpose of salvation and render His death meaningless. *Yahweh, forbid!*

Why does addressing our defaults matter? Defaults reveal our character and innermost agreements. They expose who we are under pressure. And too many have failed the test of character because they have refused to confront their defaults.

Many justify their actions, whether it be profane language, public indiscretions, or moral compromise; these responses are not accidental; they are the fruit of an unchecked appetite, their default. Corrupt communication is not random; it is cultivated over time. When priests are found cursing and speaking profanely, it is because their appetites have been fed by the world rather than purified by the Word. Some have attempted to intellectualize or justify these behaviors, but the truth is simple: *Your vacation persona is who you really are.* Who you are in private will inevitably be exposed in public, and no amount of covering will be able to hide it.

> *Yahweh is requiring a new default, one that will make us distinct disciples and a holy priesthood.*

Daniel 1-10 teaches us that *discipline develops our defaults, and our defaults create our distinction.* Daniel was a man of unshakable discipline. He was trained to have *holy* defaults, ones that did not shift based on circumstance or convenience. This level of discipline made him *distinct*. Even in captivity, he possessed the fear of the Lord and refused to compromise his posture as a son. His discipline in prayer and his refusal to defile himself set him apart.

Unfortunately, we have invited Egypt and Babylon into the temple and still expect the Glory to appear. The church has become more of a recycling bin—circulating the same people, the same patterns, and the same performances—instead of being a sacred place where true conversion happens.

Our distinction is holiness. And holiness carries weight—a just weight—a standard by which we are to live and conduct ourselves. Yet today, we often swing between extremes: either too legalistic or too liberal, both of which result in an unjust balance: *"Unequal weights are an abomination to the Lord ..."* (Proverbs 20:23 ESV).

We see a counterfeit priesthood rising—one that bears the name "church" but reflects the spirit of the age. They claim to be sons of Yahweh, but their fruit tells another story. They do not carry the marks of the Father; instead, they carry the imprint of their father, Satan. Yeshua said it plainly: *"You are of your father the devil, and your will is to do your father's desires"* (John 8:44 ESV).

This forging is not for the faint of heart. It is a call to embrace the cross—to die daily—and to be found in Him. Not having a righteousness of our own, but that which comes through faith in the Messiah (Philippians 3:9-10).

Prayer Point:

Father, forge me in the fire of Your discipline. Refine my character, and establish me as a vessel of honor, set apart for Your glory.

FORMING A PEOPLE OF HIS PRESENCE & POWER

The Commission of Devotion

Formation is the final work, the process of bringing forth something *complete*, *fit for its purpose*, and *established in its design*. The Lord is forming a people of *prayer*, *presence*, and *power*—a remnant whose intimacy with Him is *unshakable*, whose abiding is *unbroken*, and whose authority is *undeniable*.

A *praying* people is more interested in *intimacy* than *invitations*, more concerned with *consecration* than *crowds*.

Unchecked and unsubmitted desires have become dominant character traits, leading many to forsake the process of becoming. Kingdom sonship costs ... It costs you your *carnality, comfort, and character*.

Without transformation, you cannot sit in your seat of *authority* as a son. This transformation begins in *prayer*. Time spent in the presence of God grants *insight, instruction, and intimacy*. A life *drenched* in prayer is a life that *reflects the One it beholds*. However, our hunger for power, *divorced from presence*, has led many to compromise.

A *prayerless* people will always be a *presenceless* people, and the power they claim to wield is *temporal and illegal*. There remains a *standard* of holiness unto the Lord and the *fear* of the Lord, both of which are learned and acquired in the secret place of prayer.

Prayer is one of the most powerful tools and divine technologies given to the Believer, yet many neglect its development. Why? Because the *public performance of a gift* satisfies the hunger of pride, feeding the default of a heart that desires *platforms* more than *proximity*. The Bride must return to her place of *prayer* and *intense devotion to Yahweh*. Without this return, we risk repeating history—wandering in circles, drunk on our own power, believing we have found the ancient paths, only to realize we have been marching in place, going nowhere.

A life of *prayer* cultivates *discipline* and *devotion*, fine-tuning the spirit to discern truth from deception. It sharpens the senses, making us immune to the voices of the culture that have infiltrated the Body. *Prayer makes you sensitive to His presence, and it is in His presence that true power and authority are found.*

People of His *presence* are those who *dwell* in the secret place, whose lives are *marked* by the fragrance of communion, and who *carry* the reality of heaven upon the earth (Psalm 91:1; Exodus 33:13-15). Presence must always take precedence over power and demonstration.

We have become guilty of *desiring power more than we desire the One who holds it.* We have learned to stage the *appearance* of Presence—smoke, lights, production, and staging—offering a *user-friendly corporate experience* rather than an *uncompromised altar of sustainable encounter.*

We don't have to *chase* power or demonstration when we *know* the One who possesses all power. People of His presence want Him, not a performance of Him. They long to *see* His power, but they refuse to *fabricate* it. *There cannot be anything in you that says you can be bought.* Many have consulted *other gods and mediums* in Yahweh's name just to be *called powerful.* They have traded purity for platforms, authenticity for accolades, and presence for performance. *But we must have no price!*

Yahweh is *undoubtedly* forming a people of power—a people who do not merely speak of the Kingdom but demonstrate it (1 Corinthians 4:20). They walk in the authority of sons, moving in signs, wonders, and the mighty acts of God (Mark 16:17-18; Acts 1:8). This is not power for the sake of performance but power that *flows* from intimacy with Him.

> *A divine purification is sweeping through the Body, exposing the polluted altars and false demonstrations.*

It is the private pursuit that will produce the *potency* of this power on the earth. The hearts of men and women will *run to repentance*, not out of emotionalism but because true power convicts, transforms, and restores. When the Body returns to *consecration* and *communion*, we will see the *demonstration of power* fall in our gatherings as it did in times past (Acts 4:31).

There is no true power without *presence*, and there is no *sustained* presence without *prayer*. Yahweh is not calling us to *gather* for the sake of numbers or *perform* for the sake of influence—He is calling us to become a people who dwell, abide, and move in step with Him.

The *earth is groaning* for the sons of God to arise (Romans 8:19). This is the hour to return to prayer, to dwell in presence, and to walk in power. The culture will not *contaminate* this power because it is not *man-made*; it is *God-given, sent, and sustained*. The remnant will arise, and His people will be formed.

Prayer Point:

Holy Spirit, anchor my life in devotion. Let me be marked by prayer, presence, and power—for Your glory alone.

FINAL WORDS …

The call is clear. To be fashioned in *desire*, forged in *discipleship*, and formed in *devotion* is the demand of the hour. The days ahead require *a people* who have been refined in the fire of intimacy, purified in the trials of discipleship, and established in the presence of the Lord.

Let the call go forth: fashioned, forged, and formed—until He comes.

His Beloved,

Tonthalell Walters

Tonthalell Walters, a hybrid professional, is the founder of Truth And Power Ministries, Inc., Kneeology®, The Enlisted, Whole 180°, and the CEO of The Mind Box Design & Marketing Firm. With over two decades of ministry and professional experience, she bridges faith, strategy, and creativity to empower lives through coaching, branding, and transformational leadership.

Tonthalell Walters

Joy Smith

Surviving the Wilderness

The wilderness is a time in life when God intentionally draws us unto Himself. A time when He prepares us for where He is taking us. For example, this could be preparation for the next season, a future assignment, or the launching of ministry. The Father uses the time in the wilderness to remove things in us that are not reflective of His nature. Things that can be a potential stumbling block to the future. He is Alpha AND Omega, and in seeing and knowing the end of a thing, in His sovereignty, He knows what it takes for us to get there successfully. He takes the time to cultivate in us fruit that remains and to work on our character.

Here are some signs that you may be in a wilderness season:

- Warfare ensues in a way that isn't your norm.
- There is a change in provision and resources.

- Idolatry is exposed.
- Faith is tested like never before.
- There is a feeling or belief that this is just how life is going to be; from this can spring forth survival mode or the urge to make your own way.
- Temptations arise.
- Premature timing of promises or counterfeits arise.
- There is an obvious cutting away of things, even some relationships.
- There are closed doors.
- The voice of God may seem hard to discern/hear.
- You may receive unusual instructions/promptings from the Holy Spirit that you may not fully understand.

If you are experiencing several of these signs in your life, this could be an indicator that you may be entering or are currently in a wilderness season. To gain more insight on some of these indicators, let's look at some examples from biblical text.

Biblical Examples

In the wilderness, God deals with Moses and the Israelites. The children of Israel had been captive in Egypt before their promised deliverer (Moses) led them out. In the process of their deliverance and into their journey through the wilderness, God consistently showed Himself to them and the lengths that He would go to in order to win their hearts and keep His word to Abraham. *"I will cause your descendants to become as numerous as the stars of the sky, and I will give them all these lands. And through your descendants all the nations of the earth will be blessed"* (Genesis 26:4 NLT). Sometimes, when journeying through the wilderness, you may not have everything you want, but God will supply all that you need. God provided for the Israelites fresh manna daily. He made sure that their clothes and shoes never wore out. Still, they complained and reminisced about when they were in bondage and how they had "better" food then. See Numbers 11:4-6. Can you relate to this in any way? Sometimes in your wilderness, you can seek comfort of the old. It can present as an inward struggle and be unsettling. I encourage you to lean into the discomfort and see how it is there to serve you.

The Israelites also had the tendency to worship other gods. Idolatry was seen as the main cause of their downfall. I believe it is God's desire to get us to a place where, like Paul, we know how to be content in every season. Where our faith is totally in Him. Where He is God to us, and there is NO other. Where, come what may, we stand with unshakeable faith in Him, leaning not on our understanding and not being moved but what we see in the natural.

Personal Reflection

Ask yourself, what revelation is God endeavoring to unlock? What are your fears at this moment, and why? Take time to approach your loving Father in full vulnerability, knowing that this too is an invitation to deeper intimacy with Him. Search your heart during this time, and see if there is any idolatry there. This could look like idolatry of self-image, idolatry of others, idolatry of position or titles, esteeming what others think about you over your obedience to God, and more ...

Temptation Awaits

Here's another example: Right after Jesus had been announced publicly by the Father as being "His Beloved Son" in whom He was well pleased, the Holy Spirit led Jesus into the wilderness to be tempted by the devil. *"Then Jesus, full of the Holy Spirit, returned from the Jordan River. He was led by the Spirit in the wilderness, where he was tempted by the devil for forty days ..."* (Luke 4:1-2 NLT). Through each temptation of the Devil, Jesus drew from the well of the Word and wielded His sword against the enemy. He had an "It is written" ready. The Word says submit to God, resist the devil, and he will flee (James 4:7). We witness this very truth displayed here.

We can take away a few things from Jesus' wilderness experience: The wilderness is a place where you will learn the voice of God from the voice of a stranger in a greater way. You will become even more aware that there is more *for* you than *against* you. The enemy may try to take your most vulnerable moments to strike at you, but knowing and releasing the truth of the Word of God is a weapon that the enemy cannot resist! Ultimately, the wilderness set Jesus up for His next. The wilderness was the launching pad for His ministry. The wilderness served as preparation for what was to come.

Personal Reflection

What is your wilderness season preparing you for? Once you are on the other side of it, you will look back and see that what felt like it was killing you was actually birthing you into the version of yourself that was needed for your next. Meditate on Isaiah 66:9; this was a standing verse for me in one of my wilderness seasons.

How to Posture Yourself

When it comes to surviving the wilderness season, posture is key. Psalm 63 was written by David while he was in the wilderness. David ran for his life into the wilderness when Saul, someone he loved and respected, had turned against him and was trying to kill him. David was fully transparent with the Lord, and the wilderness, though hardship and testing were experienced, ultimately helped cultivate and develop his skills as a leader. This wilderness experience produced an even greater confidence, faith, and trust in God.

You can glean a few things about rightly posturing yourself from this Psalm. David knew his God and clung onto Him throughout this time like never before. You must do the same. You must lay hold of the truth of God's character. You must know what His Word says so that you know what to stand on in the midst of the emotional rollercoaster, uncertainty, and the stripping. Your flesh may cry out for other things and means of escape; the enemy may whisper lies of defeat and utterly endeavor to make you quit. But God is your source, and by posturing yourself in Him, clinging on to Him from a place of knowing He is who He says He is, you can draw strength from Him and be sustained.

If you keep reading in the story of David, you will see that those skills and the total reliance on God would be critical in his effectiveness as a leader, as he would one day become one of Israel's most important kings, defeating the Philistines, expanding Israel's territory, and becoming affectionately known as a man after God's heart.

Personal Reflection

What is your wilderness season cultivating in you? How is it linked to your destiny? What are some of the past victories you have had with God?

Sometimes, when journeying through the wilderness, it can seem that you will never get out of it. I can relate, and I promise, there is an Exodus! But rather than just focusing on the next thing, or breaking through, or the belief that things will be better if and when this happens ... Also focus on the present and lean into what God is intentionally doing in you and in your life. He desires intimacy and a greater consecration. In the wilderness, He sets you apart, and after the wilderness, He establishes you.

My Wilderness

On a personal level, in the beginning of my last wilderness season, He had me praying in tongues for at least an hour daily for a few months, and then He called me to a forty-day no food fast. I drank water with a powdered nutrient supplement for the first half of the fast and began incorporating coconut water, a juice a day, and broth before bedtime during the last half of the fast. Earlier that year, God had called me to do some radical things that required me to trust Him like never before. I did not know where we were going or how I was going to have provision. He was calling me out of the boat and, honestly, in the beginning I was afraid. As I saw His hand extended toward me in a vision, I knew He was inviting me to journey with Him to a place we had never been before. During this time, people thought I was foolish, that I didn't hear from Him, and I at times began to question His instructions. Did I really hear from God?

It was in this space where I suffered some of the greatest losses, hardships, pain, grief, uncertainty, warfare, and more. I had no idea I was in the wilderness, and I thought that I would never emerge from the seemingly low place I was in. There were times when I thought God was angry with me. I also wondered what I had done to bring about such a hard season. Sound familiar? But God had prepared me beforehand, and once I came out on the other side, I realized I had survived the wilderness. Had I known I was in the wilderness, I would have taken a different stance at times. But it was in the wilderness where the Lord met me and showed me things that were in my heart that He wanted to deal with or wanted me to surrender.

In the wilderness, I got so low and was so stripped of things, even some relationships, that all I had to cling onto was Jesus! It got to a point where I had to stop fighting the wilderness and simply surrender to it and the dealings of

God in my life. When I got to the place where I offered no resistance and fully obeyed God, there was a shift. During this time, idolatry, fear of man, pride, woundedness, doubt, bitterness, my complaining, and so much more were brought to light and dealt with. And, ultimately, I experienced an intimacy with Him and a strengthening that I never would have had I not leaned into what He was inviting me to—to know Him in ways I never had, to trust Him in ways I never had, to be healed from the inside out, and to find myself in Him.

Final Words of Encouragement

The wilderness is there to serve you. It will break you (your flesh) to build a better you. I remember feeling like I was going through a death; and I was. The Lord was killing my flesh and those things within me that were hindrances to where He was calling me to, hindrances to deeper intimacy with Him. I admonish you to fully embrace the wilderness and all that the Father has for you there. To not look at it as something that is working *against* you but rather *for* you.

To lean in and yield to the dealings of God in your life and accept the invitation he is offering - a place carved out and intentionally constructed and fashioned for you and Him. Where, if you posture yourself correctly, you can ultimately experience the nearness of the Father like never before, fully becoming aware of His sovereignty, omniscience, intentionality, beauty, faithfulness, desire for intimacy, and love and affection for you. And when you come out on the other side, which you will, you will see a glory on your life that could have only been brought forth through, and as the result of, your yielding and eventual compliance to the process that the wilderness affords you - a process of death and resurrection, breaking and fortifying, stripping and equipping, that is meant to work for you and not against you ... if you let it.

It's Time to Shift

I charge you to dust yourself off and shift your thinking and your gaze. To identify the lies that you have partnered with and renounce them. To fall out of agreement with the victim's mentality and embrace the truth, that you are an overcomer! That greater is He who is in you than He that is in the world! That God's thoughts toward you are of peace and not of evil, to give you a future and a hope! Gird yourself up, Beloved, with the Word of God, and KNOW that there is greater awaiting you on the other side. *I am rooting for you!*

> *Father, I pray for the person that is reading this right now. I thank You that You have set them apart for Yourself. That Your eyes are upon them. I thank You that You are Alpha and Omega. I thank You, God, for Your kindness, for Your sovereignty, for Your lordship over their lives, and that you are bringing them to an expected end. I thank You that You are ordering each of their steps as they journey through their wilderness season.*
>
> *I pray for more grace to be extended to them, that which would help them to lean into this Holy invitation, this set-apart place, carved out intentionally by You at this point in time in their*

lives. I pray that there would be an exchange: Let fear be exchanged for faith; let hopelessness be exchanged for hope; let resentment and bitterness be exchanged for joy; let the lies of the enemy be torn down; let Your truth and light flood their hearts; and let the peace of God be loosed against every storm in their life.

I declare that they will not journey through this season any longer than You intend them to. I declare Your timing and alignment over their lives. I declare that they will not die or give up in their wilderness but that they shall be restored and revived and receive a refreshing that carries them through to the other side.

Let Your perfect will be done concerning them, and may You receive all the Glory. In Jesus' name, Amen.

Joy Smith

Joy Smith, born in Oakland, California, is a minister, prophetic dancer, community advocate, intercessor and above all – a daughter and lover of Jesus. With fire and compassion, she stirs the weary to endure, the broken to rise, and the bride to awaken into identity, intimacy, and the fullness of Christ.

Psalmist Raine

The Missing Elements of the Righteous

To the Ecclesia of Christ Jesus our King,

I greet you in the name above every name, Jesus Christ our Lord. I am grateful for this moment to share some encouragement and intel with you that will help unify us in our outlook and perspective concerning what is happening around us. My prayer is that this will be received with an open heart and mind so that the revelation of this mandate and the standard of our King may be exemplified in how we conduct ourselves and steward the matters of this time.

These Present Times

With the conditions of this era we are in, I can imagine and, honestly, bear the same sentiments of the burdens concerning what we are facing. It is both a triumphant and a sorrowful time. I do not believe this is to bring us into a state of confusion within ourselves. I believe it is the result of our spirit man anticipating the eternal reward awaiting us. Jesus encourages us to *"Rejoice, and be exceeding glad: for great is your reward in heaven: for so persecuted they the prophets which were before you"* (Matthew 5:12 KJV).

This is the time of the unveiling of signs and wonders. This unveiling is not something you look for on the outside. It will first begin in and through you. What we often fail to realize is that in order for this unveiling to happen, opportunities must present themselves that probe the necessity of its solution. This thought can come with a warning to brace yourself; but do not be afraid. You only want to gird yourself for what else could come. Although I can imagine your weariness regarding matters of despair and circumstances, we are reminded throughout the Holy Scriptures not to forfeit the eternal place for temporary satisfaction or relief.

The Apostle Paul reminded the church of Corinth, *"... do not lose heart. Even though our outward man is perishing, yet the inward man is being renewed day by day. For our light affliction, which is but for a moment, is working for us a far more exceeding and eternal weight of glory, while we do not look at the things which are seen, but at the things which are not seen. For the things which are seen are temporary, but the things which are not seen are eternal"* (2 Corinthians 4:16-18 NKJV).

As a Body, I have seen too many of us unaware of how our tests and trials will show up to produce. This is a key missing element amongst the righteous. It is our duty to see every moment and opportunity the way that Christ sees it so we can steward these opportunities in a greater way. It costs us too much to remain unaware. We need to ask the Lord, "What will this moment, this test, this trial yield?" The moment we feel conflict, we typically lose our stance in hope. But even in this, we are not without hope. We are holding onto a promise, a goal, and that is the fuel behind our endurance. We are hopeful and in great joy about seeing our King face-to-face, and all of what we are facing will soon be a forgotten thought. For that glory that is before us is so much greater than what we are facing now.

Missing Element 1: Our Response

With all that has been shared, I need you to know that our endurance is a massive part of our response in these dire times. Not only are we not looking at our trials as opportunities but we are also not enduring to see the fruit at the end. In this hour, your endurance matters, and it is a key element for the righteous. Even as God's word declares, *"Let us not grow weary in our well doing, for we will reap if we faint not"* (Galatians 6:9 KJV). There are many that are looking for hope, refuge, and solutions. Many are searching for answers that we know our God possesses, which at moments can be concealed; but the Lord reveals them as the kings search them out (Proverbs 25:2).

This means that we have a responsibility to respond to these times. As sons of God and representatives of the Kingdom of God on Earth, we cannot sit and just observe the conditions of this world and watch it all crumble. There are souls that need salvation and an Earth that we must tend to for our time remaining here. This was our original mandate as man (Genesis 2:15). Of course, we had come to a fallen state and allowed sin to continue to rip us further from the original instructions entrusted to us by God. We had really lost sight of our charge to steward this Earth well. God created and planted us in this place. We are required to steward this place for His Glory. The burden of my heart has been, *Father, forgive us for getting so far from our assignment.*

Now, we can dwell in condemnation about that, but it would not be the appropriate response. It is our righteous duty, as followers of Christ Jesus and citizens of His Kingdom, to take up our cross and follow Him (Luke 9:23). We do this with great honor and with our entire heart and mind set to bestow glory on the One who took our place on the cross at Calvary. This is our initial response. We cannot respond righteously on Earth without understanding the very source and fuel of our response. It is for the glory of Him who was found worthy to take our place. Forsaking this element as a righteous one would cost us in the sight of the Lord. With this intention at the core of our actions, we make room for great and marvelous things to happen on Earth. I want to encourage you to secure and purify your intentions. Let your endurance be ignited as a response for what He has done for you. This is your testimony. This is your witness on Earth.

To add to this thought, the world is not too crowded with those giving Jesus Christ the honor that is due. For no one can respond as a witness for you. Many can make an account and strong witness about you, but no one can take the place of extending gratitude on your behalf like you can. He died for you. He was raised to life for you. For you, it was a demonstration of the power of an endless life (Hebrews 7:16). So, set your heart to show up in strength and in courage for the ONE you believe in and the ONE who believes in you. Many vow to live their lives dedicated to not acknowledging Him; but He is the stamp of Glory on our lives. I know the pain of the era seems unbearable at times. I know the things that we are facing seem tremendously unexplainable, unbelievable even; but your witness is such a strong response to His redemption on your behalf.

So, I admonish you to respond well. Respond well in your endurance. Respond well in your seeking. Respond well in your diligence to be a witness for Him. Respond well by hiding and not dimming your light. For this light shines through your good works and causes men to glorify the Father, which is in Heaven (Matthew 5:16).

As your sister and co-laborer in Christ, I would not have you be ignorant, thinking that the enemy will not try to pervert your perspective of this bright, shining light through you. Letting that light shine brightly is not a way to make you a target, like some have come to believe. Letting that light shine is a part of His Glory being released upon men (Revelations 21:23-26). It is a solution in the darkness. Jesus gave us this light, which is exposed through our life and living. The scriptures say that He (Jesus) is the light of men, and darkness cannot comprehend it. Could you imagine that the overall solution to this time of darkness is His Light? It can only be shined through those who receive and have believed in Jesus Christ. He is the only one who can give you this light (John 1:4-5).

Now, I will warn you that the imitator, our adversary, makes every attempt to trap those who persevere. He makes attempts to produce a false light. For the Scriptures say, "... *And no wonder! For Satan himself transforms himself into an angel of light. Therefore it is no great thing if his ministers also transform themselves into ministers of righteousness, whose end will be according to their works*" (2 Corinthians 11:14-15 NKJV).

We have to grow in fellowship with the Lord Jesus Christ so that we are able to discern between Christ's light and a false light that is presenting itself on Earth. This is one of the most important aspects of our response in this critical hour. For there are many believers who are being easily deceived. There are many who are waiting in the balance of confusion, which is bringing their impact to a halt. There are those who have chosen to sit on the sidelines of these times because of the whirlwind of delusion and deceit. Although I understand and even empathize with the weight of this factor, I cannot encourage us enough to ensure that we draw closer to the Lord in such a greater way in this time. It is our devotion and God's molding through this process that will allow us to be sensitive to what is presented before us. We cannot afford to fall away due to this weakness of the flesh.

Missing Element 2: The Time of Solutions

We truly need to set our hearts on growing in the truth of the Lord that leads us along the paths of His truth. The path of truth and righteousness will allow us to birth and release solutions on Earth, even amidst the pressures of this time. When things are critical like this, it is the most potent time for the release of heavenly answers. New pathways are created; hope arises in such unique ways. The salvation of the Lord through this is revealed to a world which is looking for a solution.

It amazes me how the missing element of the intentional administration of this time is not recognized. If we really recognized what was needed in this time, we would understand the need to be solutionists. The truth is that God released us in this time for the specific purpose of bringing and being a solution on Earth while we are here. We only have a bit of time, for our life is but a vapor. (James 4:14)

Yet in the Lord's faithfulness, He will provide all with an opportunity to receive this salvation found through His son, Jesus. As the Scriptures state, *"The Lord is not slack concerning His promise, as some count slackness, but is longsuffering toward us, not willing that any should perish but that all should come to repentance"* (2 Peter 3:9 NKJV).

In all of this, I need you to know that this is marked as one of the greatest times for the Ecclesia. We will see our King reign triumphantly, with our enemy completely defeated once and for all and the government of our God's Kingdom established stronger in such a greater way for all to see, even until eternity.

I pray that you will rise to the occasion and dedicate your life from this point forward to fill whatever gaps are missing toward this call. This call to fill gaps is also a call to be able to identify your grace and move in that. This is not a call to take the world on your shoulders. The Lord has staffed this world with those that need to be awakened to their grace and calling so they can assist in filling the voids. To the one who struggles with carrying the weight of God's burdens, He has not put more on you than what you can bear. Even if you can see and feel the need, even if you are praying for the solutions, He won't put more on you than what you can do. He actually built our capacity. Trust His wisdom in this. Let Him guide you on what you can do and pray until the voids are filled in the rest. This is the only way to remain faithful and not negligent.

Other Missing Elements

There are also other valuable elements that are necessary but missing out of our norms, such as truth, courage, devotion, determination, awareness, and solution-orientation. These are all necessary components for us to endure victoriously in this time. With our eyes set on the Lord, we will yield to the weight and impact of His move in this time. All of this is for the purpose of seeing His Glory truly revealed. We are all stepping up to the plate, and I look forward to seeing this victory coming to pass for the Ecclesia on Earth.

Father, you have set chosen ones on Earth to purposefully serve and demonstrate the reality of your Kingdom on Earth. You have called, and they have answered, surrendering their lives to your move on Earth. Although the warfare has been intensed, we are confident that we are equipped for this work. Keep us in Your will, Holy Father. Keep our hearts anchored in You so that we are not wavering in our faith. We will seek after Your will continuously so that we may move in the revelation of Your truth. For it is in Your truth that we are free, and whom the Son has set free, he is truly free indeed. Thank You for this move of Your Spirit amongst Your Ecclesia on Earth, in Jesus' name. Amen!

Psalmist Raine

Psalmist Raine is an apostolic voice, author, shepherd, wife, and mother with a passion to empower the Body of Christ with truth through encounters and tools that transform lives, restoring and refreshing our original God-designed DNA. She is renowned worldwide as a worship leader, but she is a vessel that God uses to release His heart for the Kingdom.

Earlye Julien

Beware of Distractions

Key Scripture:
Colossians 2:8 (The Passion Translation, TPT)

Greetings from Earlye Julien, a Servant of Christ

Greetings in the name of our Savior, Lord, and King, Jesus Christ. I am a servant who has been charged to glorify God, to share the Good News of Jesus Christ to dying souls, to serve this present age, and to leave a legacy for the next. Though I have longed to fulfill this charge for a very long time, it was necessary that I spend time developing my faith and growing in the grace and knowledge of our Lord and Savior Jesus Christ.

So, the vision tarried until this appointed time. Finally, I am compelled with all the power that is within me to keep this charge and have begun to cultivate it now, by writing to you.

Greetings from My Fellow Laborers in Christ

I also extend greetings to you from my fellow laborers in Christ, Elisha, Allana, Tonthalell, Joy, Lizbeth, Alissia, and Lisa. We have labored together with Apostle Psalmist Raine to encourage you in your faith. The Apostle Paul beseeched us many years ago in 2 Corinthians 3:1-3 (NLT) to live our lives as living letters so that everyone can see and recognize the Spirit of the Living God in and through our lives. Therefore, rather than focusing on letters to be read and commended, we have devoted ourselves to living out our faith in a way that people can see our good works as we strive to become lovers of the Word and more and more like Christ. This did not happen overnight. It took much preparation.

What can now be seen *outwardly* was *cultivated inwardly* through 1) weekly, intentional time studying the Word of God together; 2) prayer and meditation; and 3) quality seek time in God's presence, where He transformed each of us by the renewing of our minds during those sacred conversations with Him. Many of you have read about those sacred conversations, as Apostle Raine encouraged us to scribe highlights for your benefit. We hoped that when you read how amazing it has been for us, you would be encouraged to intentionally schedule your own allotted time for sacred conversations with God.

News Regarding Our Recent Commissions

Each of us is fulfilling our calling in different ways, both inside and outside the walls of our churches, within the United States and abroad. We are grateful to Apostle Raine, the visionary who formed the "Morning Meets with God" community of believers. Though God has already accomplished in us more than we imagined, Apostle Raine has remained vigilant about meeting regularly together with God to trim our lamps and build ourselves up in the Spirit so we don't run out of oil. She has fostered a revival in us not only to study the Word but to become true lovers of the Word. Further, she has emphasized the importance of obedience to carry out God's instructions and display what the Spirit has written in our hearts as living letters.

Now, the time has come when we have been released to share the message of our living letters that God has given each of us for you.

Greetings to My Brothers and Sisters in Christ

I am writing to you, my brothers and sisters in Christ (individually and collectively) who have labored so diligently to build on the foundation of the Apostles and Prophets with Jesus Christ as the Cornerstone.

Acknowledgment of Your Achievements

I rejoice with you regarding your achievements. I have heard about your great faith in Jesus Christ, your enduring love for one another, and your compassionate and benevolent love for others. Your ministries have prospered and reached the hearts of many people. As a result, many all over the world have given their hearts to Jesus Christ and have allowed Him to be Lord over their lives. These are the magnetic characteristics that compelled me to seek to know Christ for myself.

Some of you have devoted yourselves to discipling one person at a time, some to small groups, and others minister to hundreds or thousands. You have built beautiful buildings and organized community outreach and mission groups to extend all over the world. You have accomplished many great things that your ancestors would have never dreamed possible. Again, I rejoice with you!

Acknowledgment of Your Frustrations

I have also heard of your frustrations regarding challenges you faced during the COVID-19 pandemic, which resulted in some long-haul negative effects and unintended consequences. In your sincere efforts to advance in spite of your frustrations, you developed countless new programs. You incorporated the wisdom of multicultural ideas to foster inclusiveness, intermingling old and new approaches. To be relevant with this present age, you released many old traditions and implemented new ones. Each of you learned to multitask. You became more self-sufficient, which allowed you to accomplish more individually and reduced the need for group engagement. You educated yourselves in the mindset and logic of the world's systems and engaged in the use of technology to bring your ministries to people all over the world. Where you were once single-minded in focus, you have each evolved into multifaceted phenomena.

Where you were once distinctly different and set apart from the world, you were forced to find ways to be more relatable and incorporate practices to prevent you from being totally disconnected from the world and each other. Unfortunately, some of the very people who intimidated you into some form of assimilation now claim to be confused by you. They claim to find Christians indistinguishable from non-Christians. And, to your surprise, the endeavors you so desperately hoped would lead to immense progression in knowing Christ and making Him known have unintentionally and sadly resulted in distracting you away from God's intended purpose.

Many nights I have wept and prayed with much compassion for you. I have prayed, understanding the immense sacrifices you have made and the loneliness and isolation you often feel. I understand the time management and financial struggles you face. I understand the increasingly complex societal issues (unemployment, homelessness, poverty, crime, substance abuse, mental and physical health, political and cultural issues, etc.) that plague your mind. I understand the constant overload of media and social media information and misinformation. I understand the plight of depending on

God while working with undependable people. I understand your heart's desire to please God while fighting the demand to please people. I understand when your cries to God have seemingly gone unheard and the weariness that comes when passion converges with burnout. Indeed, I have prayed for you from a position of understanding. But I want to encourage you with Biblical wisdom and strategies.

Paul's Warning

Paul, in his prophetic, infamous wisdom, cautioned us:

> *"Beware that no one distracts you or intimidates you in their attempt to lead you away from Christ's fullness by pretending to be full of wisdom when they're filled with endless arguments of human logic. For they operate with humanistic and clouded judgments based on the mindset of this world system, and not the anointed truths of the Anointed One"* (Colossians 2:8 TPT).

Paul's prophetic caution was spot-on. Many of you who were once laser-focused only on Jesus and Him crucified, lending your ear only to the Holy Spirit, have become distracted, as Paul perceived you might. You have adopted world philosophies and human logic as wisdom instead of the Truth in the Word of God. Jesus sacrificed His life to set you free from the foolery of this world, yet you have embraced it.

I would love to tell you that what the Spirit has placed on my heart comes from the trouble I avoided by strictly heeding

Paul's warning. Unfortunately, I am compelled to write this letter out of the pain I have suffered from my mistakes. Unintentionally at first, I was lured by worldly temptations and found myself justifying worldly wisdom and logic over Godly wisdom, Biblical Truth, and devotion to God alone. I failed to beware of the distractions. It is my hope that you will learn from my experience.

Distractions

1 Peter 5:8 (NLT) admonishes us to *"Stay alert! Watch out for your great enemy, the devil. He prowls around like a roaring lion, looking for someone to devour."* One of Satan's most effective strategies for taking your focus off God and the plans He has for you is the use of distractions. A distraction is anything that "directs one's attention away from something else" (Merriam Webster Dictionary).

The sources of distractions are too numerous to name, and they vary from person to person. However, I've listed some common ones that may have served to distract you from stewarding wisely over your God ordained time, responsibilities, resources, and purpose.

Common Sources of Distractions and How to Overcome Them

1. *SMARTPHONES AND OTHER ELECTRONICS*
   Our devices—phones, tablets, TVs—offer constant connection but often at the cost of spiritual focus. With nonstop notifications and endless scrolling, we become easy targets for distraction.

The Distraction
Excessive use turns helpful tools into idols. Studies show many check their phones every 12 minutes, with nearly half of Americans showing signs of addiction.

The Truth
These tools aren't evil in themselves—but when they dominate our attention, we risk missing God's voice.

The Response
Practice self-control. Set boundaries on screen time. Use technology as a servant, not a master.

Hide this Word in your heart
"[Looking away from all that will distract us and] focusing our eyes on Jesus, who is the Author and Perfecter of faith [the first incentive for our belief and the One who brings our faith to maturity] ..." (Hebrews 12:2 AMP).

2. *PEOPLE*
   The voices around us—friends, coworkers, even family—can influence our decisions and distract us from God's plan.

   The Distraction
   People may mean well, but their opinions often conflict with God's will. Constantly seeking approval can lead us away from His purpose.

   The Truth
   God's counsel must outweigh human advice. Your loyalty belongs to His voice first.

The Response
Seek Spirit-led counsel. Make space for God's voice to be the loudest in your life.

Hide this Word in your heart
"This is what the Lord says: 'Cursed are those who put their trust in mere humans, who rely on human strength and turn their hearts away from the Lord'" (Jeremiah 17:5 NLT).

3. *WORLDLY INFLUENCES*
   The world around us pressures us to conform—to fit in, follow trends, and chase success at all costs.

   The Distraction
   Worldly ideas may seem harmless, but compromise leads to spiritual decline. What seems right may lead to death (Proverbs 14:12).

   The Truth
   We are called to be set apart. God's Word must shape our values, not culture.

   The Response
   Be transformed by renewing your mind. Filter every influence through the truth of Scripture.

   Hide this Word in your heart:
   "Don't copy the behavior and customs of this world, but let God transform you ..." (Romans 12:2 NLT)

4. *CHASING SUCCESS*
   Ambition can be good—but not when it pulls us away from God's direction.

   The Distraction
   When we define success by worldly standards, we may miss God's will. Striving can replace surrender.

   The Truth
   True success is found in obedience. God's definition often looks different from ours.

   The Response
   Seek God first. Trust Him to lead, provide, and promote in His timing.

   Hide this Word in your heart
   "But seek first the kingdom of God and His righteousness, and all these things shall be added to you" (Matthew 6:33 NKJV).

5. *NEGATIVE THOUGHTS, FEELINGS, AND ATTITUDES*
   Fear, offense, hopelessness, and bitterness can quietly consume our inner world.

   The Distraction
   These aren't just emotions—they're spiritual distractions rooted in unresolved heart issues.

   The Truth
   God desires to heal your heart. His truth brings clarity and peace.

The Response
Ask God to search your heart (Psalm 139:23–24). Trust His promises, no matter what you feel.

Hide this Word in your heart:
"for we walk by faith, not by sight [living our lives in a manner consistent with our confident belief in God's promises]" (2 Corinthians 5:7 AMP).

Your Action Plan to Overcome Distractions

1. Ask God to search your heart and reveal to you anything that by your words, actions, deeds, failure to act, or investment of time, take priority over Him.
2. Make a list of the distractions in your life that take you off focus.
3. What can you do this week to mitigate each one of those distractions, remove them altogether, or at least limit them from stealing your time, talent, resources, efforts, and energy away from God?

I Have Prayed for You

I give thanks to God for you and have prayed earnestly for you. I have prayed that you will grow stronger in your faith. I have prayed that you will recognize the signs before distractions creep into your life or your ministries. I have prayed that you will be repulsed by the things of this world and crave only the things of God. I have prayed that you will be *"steadfast, immovable, always abounding in the work of the Lord, knowing that your labor is not in vain in the Lord"* (1 Corinthians 15:58 NKJV). Finally, I have prayed that as you seek God and His righteousness first, He will give you the desires of your heart and bring you much success.

Pray for Me

Just as I have prayed for you, I ask that you pray for me too! Pray that God will continue to give me opportunities to share the Gospel of Jesus Christ, and when He does, that I will proclaim it with boldness, as I should. Pray that I will continue to live my life as a living letter among both those who know Christ and those who do not. Pray that God will continue to impart Godly wisdom and strategies that I may in turn impart to you as a modern-day scribe. And, most importantly, pray that I will remain laser-focused, avoiding the distractions that the Apostle Paul warned us about.

Final Encouragement

Just as the Apostle Paul encouraged the church of Colossae to pass on his letters, I likewise, encourage you. After you have read this letter and the other letters by my fellow laborers in Christ, pass them on to others so they can read them, too. And when you do, encourage them to get focused. Caution them to avoid distractions that have been planted by the enemy to kill, steal, and destroy destinies.

I will write more to you soon about the specific charge God has given me to keep to glorify Him. I am committed to encourage you so you will be inspired to carry out all that the Lord has purposed you to do. So, be on the lookout for the next project God has purposed me to scribe for you. To God be the glory, He who is able to strengthen you, keep you, and bless you indeed!

Yours in Christ,

Earlye Julien

Earlye Julien is passionate about writing to encourage and uplift the Body of Christ to overcome obstacles, deepen their faith, and advance the Kingdom of God. She has earned master's degrees in counseling and educational administration and serves alongside her husband as campus pastor of River City Church, Uptown Campus in Moline, IL.

Psalmist Raine

The Ministry of Worship

Great grace be upon the righteous nation of our King Jesus Christ, who reigns triumphantly as King of Kings. It is my greatest honor to share with you an unveiling of a great key in the very foundation of our stance in this hour. I come by no other authority than that which has been laid upon me by our Lord and Savior Jesus Christ. Being commissioned by the Lord to labor in the field, I share just a small piece of the burden regarding the conditions of our lives as it pertains to our lives of worship. I am not referring to what we have minimized worship to. As we should know and I cannot stress enough, worship is not about gifts and talents.

Our worship is the very essence of our existence and should be in service toward the audience of One in our life.

Worship is a life that exemplifies the worth of God in one's life through adoration, reverence, and complete obedience.

The standards of worship that reflect the worth of God have not been maintained as they should have been. For our God is Holy—being blameless, without spot or blemish, set apart, whole, and *perfect*. In accordance with the Holy Scriptures in 1 Peter, the standard for us is: Just as He is, we should be also. This is not something we can obtain on our own. There is no ability or determination of mind that will allow us to, first, fathom what that standard is like alone and, second, execute something that is completely by the Spirit of the Living God. It takes the Lord's molding and our submission to His processes for us to reflect Him on Earth. We are to grow to the full measure of our Savior Jesus Christ (Ephesians 4:13). He is our model and our example for life and living. However, if we struggle with the targeted purpose of our actions, we will run the risk of fulfilling a purpose without care or any thought of honor.

This is how falsehood is birthed. It develops without proper regard toward the intent and purposes of what God has originally put in place. This opens the doors for delusion, perversion, and deceit. It has always been the intent of God for us to know and dwell in His presence. He has been adamant about building His habitation among us. Even in tumultuous times, He desires for you to know and live in the fact that He is with you. This calls us to live in ways that can impact our world around us. Some of us have lived in very risky ways, and the Lord has prevented dangers from approaching your life and the life of those who are connected to you, without you even knowing. God has given mercy, and we did not even know we were in need of it. However, if we made it our business to live in a way that makes room for Him to dwell, the very essence of His presence in our midst is enough to sustain our lives for the greater. So, what I need us to acknowledge is that there is no greater way to welcome the presence of the Lord in your life than to live a life that makes room for Him through worship.

Over time, our actions and routines in worship have revealed that we have lost sight of the ministry of worship. Worship has never been about ministry to ourselves, but to the Lord. It amazes me when I see how far we have gotten away from the very essence of this. We have used every element of this ministry to serve our insecurities and ambitions and to make us feel better, when in fact our actions and our life of worship was always destined to serve the Lord.

Could it be that since we have not focused on ministering to Him, we have accidentally "X'd" Him out of our lives? I can only imagine the dominion effect of His absence. When we pushed God away from the focus of our ministry of worship, we pushed out our security, our anchoring of heart and mind, and our stability. We are seeing the fruit of it across our world. The condition of our world is not only impacted by our decisions but also by our life of worship. We, as God's people, have become chameleons on Earth. Many cannot tell us apart from the world. We have lost our voice, our influence. We have shown that we cannot stand in the midst of crisis. We have become unreliable as a refuge and a center for solutions for our world because we have left our primary ministry.

I want to encourage you to reclaim your state and never forget your ministry of worship. It is not about a corporate move. It is a personal decision. It is more important in this time than ever before. It is in this hour when we have to stand for something, or we will fall for anything. It is through your life of worship that your stance will be solidified. There is a position and a post in this ministry of worship that has been a major factor that has sustained and preserved our minds, our families, and even the nations we live in. We cannot afford to forsake our post. This post and service was a mandate of ministry that, at one point in time, was set aside for only an elected few. Now, since Christ was crucified for the redemption of the world, the mandate is for everyone that has committed their life to Him. This mandate can be found in 1 Peter 2.

> *"Coming to Him as to a living stone, rejected indeed by men, but chosen by God and precious, you also, as living stones, are being built up a spiritual house, a holy priesthood, to offer up spiritual sacrifices acceptable to God through Jesus Christ."* (1 Peter 2:4-5 NKJV).

> *"But you are a chosen generation, a royal priesthood, a holy nation, His own special people, that you may proclaim the praises of Him who called you out of darkness into His marvelous light; who once were not a people but are now the people of God, who had not obtained mercy but now have obtained mercy"* (1 Peter 2:9-10 NKJV).

This is now the dispensation where we are established as a priestly nation, also known as the priesthood. Anyone who accepts and believes the Lord Jesus has been called to this mandate and post (Revelation 1:6; Revelation 5:9-10). This is a new reality of life for those that believe. Becoming a new creature was something we have always shared, but having a new order of life has been something we have not announced. This is our light in a dark world. If our ministry remains in truth—pure and potent—we will house the very presence of the Lord. All of our help, all of our hope, all of our provision is in Him. As a result, nations can be transformed, cities can be redeemed, and families can be restored. Overall order, God's order, can be reset on Earth. Although massive in outlook, this transformation happens one vessel at a time, one decision at a time. All it takes is for one to be on their post—yielding to the ministry of worship unto the Lord.

Priestly Mandate

In order to live out what it means to be a priestly nation, we need to understand the mandate for the priesthood. This mandate carries our identity. The priestly mandate is for the nature of the King-Priest to arise in every believer. Established after the order of Melchizedek, this identity marker was established even before the dispensation of the law. It was an order of life that Abraham, the father of many nations, would revere (Genesis 14:17-20). As a result of this act of reverence, all nations have yielded to this order (Hebrews 7:4-10).

This King-Priest function requires us to take a look at Joshua. In Zechariah 6, Joshua was crowned by the order of the Lord. He was charged to build the temple, to bear the glory of the Lord, and to sit and rule from His throne. He was also charged to serve as a priest from His throne. The Holy Scriptures commanded harmony between the two roles and duties. In our present day, we have not seen a godly model of this function. We have seen the priestly role and the governing role separate. We have lived in the reality that these roles would conflict. We have set it as such a mandate for living that there are many who believe in the separation of church and state. We have had governing laws that support that reality, but is that really the way of the Lord?

Since the exodus of the nation of Israel, God has always called forward a nation that lives under the governance of the presence of God. This priestly mandate of this hour brings us back to God's heart concerning this design amongst His children. How did we get so far away from this? This could only be as a result of comparing our lives to the lives of other nations. Our envy of other nations could cause us to dismiss the open heavens we are supposed to live under. Even with what we see before our eyes, the destruction of the nations around us does not have to be the destruction of God's people. Psalm 91:8 states that only with our eyes will we see the reward of the wicked.

It may appear on the surface that the wicked and godless nations are prospering or excelling beyond those who are of this Holy Nation, but soon, and very soon, will they see who has never lost a battle. It is our King, who will defeat our adversaries right before our eyes. May we be the nation that stands strong in the battle of the end times. Our decisions, commitment, and worship today can impact our victory tomorrow. You cannot allow the pressure of these times to push you to a place of abandoning your ministry of worship. Many have allowed oppression and opportunities to cause them to forfeit their vow and commitment to God. You have to build a strong commitment to the Lord regardless of the pressures opposed. As the Scriptures encourage us, "... having done all to stand. Stand therefore ..." (Ephesians 6:13-14 NKJV). This is the hour to truly stand. We cannot afford to repeat the history of those who had been called as the Children of God.

Presence-Based Governance

Even now, wherever you may be, every action you make, whether you are leading a pack, a member of a pack, or your environment is calling for a change, you are there for the purposes of making a difference. We are world changers. We are called to change our world, one decision, one yes, one move of obedience at a time. Every single one of our actions impacts something for someone else. Every decision impacts another person or circumstances, whether it seems to be for the good or not. Due to this issue, we cannot afford to make changes based on our preferences or our emotions. It is too costly.

We cannot make changes and decisions based on our voids. We must make changes and decisions based on the guidance and the leadership of the Holy Spirit. Jesus left this realm called Earth so that this gift could come to us. As acknowledged by Jesus in John 16, it was necessary for the Holy Spirit to come to guide us, to teach us, to make us aware of what is coming. With the intel and wisdom that we receive from the Holy Spirit, we are entrusted to live our life in accordance with that exchange. The Lord does not intend for us to be puffed up with knowledge, doing nothing with what we have heard. We have been charged according to the Scriptures to be doers of His word and not just hearers only. How we live and what we build from that will impact the world around us. The fruit of this exchange will be global transformation.

This is what we are responsible for—Global Transformation. We have been marked as guardians of this world. This has been our mandate since the Lord established us in this realm in Genesis.

> *"This is the history of the heavens and the earth when they were created, in the day that the Lord God made the earth and the heavens, before any plant of the field was in the earth and before any herb of the field had grown. For the Lord God had not caused it to rain on the earth, and there was no man to till the ground; but a mist went up from the earth and watered the whole face of the ground ... The Lord God planted a garden eastward in Eden, and there He put the man whom He had formed"* (Genesis 2:4-6, 8 NKJV).

God's design has always been presence-based governance. We were placed on Earth to tend to it, to steward this realm in the presence of the Lord. Adam moved and operated as a governor of this land God placed him in, being surrounded by the presence of the Lord. This has been our duty and model from the beginning. Our redemption brought us back to that duty and even to that expectation. We live to reclaim what has been lost. In every move, we reclaim and return to our original duty. Can you imagine how that would please the Lord?

So, while we are in this space, while we have this opportunity, let us live in the reality of this redemption. You are not meant to lose this opportunity again. Let us live in service to the Lord, where we live in the restoration of His order. He is perfect in all of His ways, full of splendor and grace. Where we mismanaged before, we will no longer mismanage. Regardless of the circumstances that have brought us to this moment, it is now time for us to arise. We cannot afford to not operate in the way God has called us to. It is in our makeup. It is in our DNA.

So, I charge you to arise. The only way out of these obstacles is to step up. Step up to the occasion. Step up and birth the solution. Step up and create the new pathways—innovate. Step up and produce fruit that remains. Step up and release the glory of the Lord.

This is the way to govern while we are yet here on the Earth. This is the mandate of the Ecclesia—the Governing Assembly of the Lord Jesus Christ.

May this mandate be sealed in your hearts. No matter the time or the season. Your makeup has been built for this work of governing this realm according to the will of the

Lord. While you are on this Earth, I charge you to fulfill this mandate and bring the Glory of the Lord back to this Earth. I stand as a witness to see this impact on Earth, but I do not stand alone. There is a whole cloud of witnesses standing awaiting this reality to be made active on Earth. Let us serve the Lord with gladness and bring Him delight. This is our reasonable service.

Psalmist Raine

Lizbeth Pioquinto

A Steady Trust

To you, believer, who finds yourself reading this letter in the midst of changing times: Remember to stand firm with the help of God the Father and the Lord Jesus Christ, our Savior. Grace, mercy, and peace.

We are living in times when we see that everything happens very quickly. What is today, can change tomorrow or in a moment. This can be seen in current situations, such as in technology, weather, family, personal relationships, and even global events like wars. Most of these changes can lead to a lack of trust.

A very practical example: In terms of technology, our devices require an update from time to time; otherwise, they start not working properly. Believe it or not, this can disrupt life for a moment (work, school, ministry, global, and other areas) by preventing us from communicating, getting to the right place on time, etc.

In your personal life, when you require this "update" for peace,trust amid uncertainty, what then?

The answer is found in truly loving God's Word, God's Truth. Make it the foundation of your existence and your posture; position toward it. I'm sharing with you what I have lived, and God confirms it to me according to His Word through #MMwG.

In His Word, In His Truth

There is no other way; in the midst of changes, God remains immutable and trustworthy to His Word. This leads to being the only true source for the update (peace, trust) that you may need in life because God does not lie (Matthew 24:35 NKJV; Hebrews 6:16-20 AMP; John 17:17 NKJV; Titus 1:2 NKJV).

It is vital that you have a relationship with God, inquire about Him in what is happening and what you are living, hearing, and seeing. Don't be easily fooled, moved, or disturbed in your thinking. Go to Him through His Word and in prayer. When He gives you His answer, respond to Him in obedience with the sole motivation of giving, rendering to Him what He is asking for. There will be times when His response confronts your beliefs, opinions, feelings, and understanding, which may not align with His Word. It is at that point that your heart must decide to surrender to His truth. In doing so, you assure and protect yourself from offering deception to Him and deceiving yourself. Otherwise, you run the risk of God allowing you to believe your own lie as a consequence:

condemnation and suffering, even total separation from Him. Perhaps the struggles you are going through (the example I have given of the need for peace and trust) are because you need to correct where His Word is pointing. Align yourself by loving and accepting the truth that He is teaching you; it is God showing His love and giving you the opportunity to correct. When He makes His will known to you, He will help you frame some answers (worlds, realities, His truth) by faith and in prayer, built on a strong foundation since it is based on the truth of His Word. With certainty and conviction, you will see the results brought to reality, legislating in accordance with His will.[a]

You realize that this steady trust is not obtained through your relationships with people. It is not wrong to have relationships, but this trust is obtained through your relationship with God through Jesus Christ, regardless of what is happening, and in total dependence on Him. This attitude of the heart, toward His Truth spoken by His Spirit to your spirit or by His written Word, will keep you in a posture and position that is acceptable to God, enabling you to move forward in His plans and purposes, that is, in His will.

Be determined to do it, just as Jesus remained determined to obey, to surrender to the Father's will, and to set His face like a flint even in uncomfortable, painful situations, in the midst of persecution and judgment, knowing that He would not be shamed.[b]

Focused and obedient, demonstrating the love of the Father that He has for all of us, He offers to save us from the punishment we deserve, giving us the opportunity to know

Him, the only true God, and Jesus Christ whom He sent. This means living eternal life from here on Earth, receiving His love and peace that surpasses all understanding and trusting in Him because He has overcome the world.

He has taught and shown me in more detail how, when I trust in what He has spoken and inquire before Him about His will (believing in faith that God hears in prayer, structuring through His Word worlds, realities, and His truth), to see His grace in family situations. I want to share this with you: After some time praying that a close family member could go to college, we prayed and thanked God for the opportunity, even though it was not yet a reality. Then, one day, the school called a meeting. All the teachers were there, and the counselor congratulated the family member and gave us the news that he had been nominated for a scholarship.

Speaking the Word and truth of God over him, we prayed that he would be strong, of good spirit, and diligent in his studies. Now, he is living the reality of attending college through a prepaid scholarship. At some point God spoke into this young man's life, giving him direction through His spoken Word by His Spirit to his spirit; this is being fulfilled for the glory of God. Also, in other areas, such as serving in church and regarding severe weather situations in the state where I reside, to the glory of God, I was able to live out the solution. Sometimes, confronted by His response, yes, it has been necessary to correct myself in the middle of the process to see His grace and mercy, for which I'm grateful.

God is real, and in Him, it is possible to live confidently, loving His Word of truth and accepting the true message of

Jesus Christ. Come before Him with transparency, without fear or shame. When He shows you something in your life that is not aligned with His Word, do not be offended; be grateful. He shows this to correct and align you with His truth. Let us obey; His Word quickens us; He is perfecting our lives. There are no shortcuts; only God, through Jesus Christ, His Word, gives life to our spirit, and the Spirit gives life. The words God gives you are from the Spirit and give life. Outside of this truth that comes from God, there is no other because everything else cannot give us a healthy faith that helps us live eternal life from here on Earth, fulfilling His will. He has given us His Spirit to strengthen and guide us. Believe and hold on to His Word; it is trustworthy (John 6:63 ERV, AMPC).

May you be a living letter so that others can read and know the true answer to a steady trust: *"For this is good and acceptable in the sight of God our Savior, who desires all men to be saved and to come to the knowledge of the truth. For there is one God and one Mediator between God and men, the Man Christ Jesus, ..."* (1 Timothy 2:3-5 NKJV).

Father, in the name of Jesus, I present the reader of this letter to You. Lord, I ask that, with the help of Your Word and Holy Spirit, they come to a true encounter with You, where their lives are impacted by Your love. May they, upon deciding to trust in and do Your Word, live out Your answer to the situation they are going through. Transform and continually align their lives with Your Truth, Your Word, Your Son Jesus as they stand firm, fulfilling Your perfect will. Amen.

For His glory and honor.

Lizbeth Pioquinto

REFERENCES

(a) John 16:13-15 NKJV; 2 Thessalonians 2:10 NKJV; Hebrews 11:1-3 AMP. Friday AM (1.3.25) Seek Session.

(b) Lamp Day (1.15.25) 1 Peter 1:1-10 NLT, KJV; Lamp Day (12.4.24) Isaiah 50:4-7 NLT, KJV; 1 Timothy 1:18-19 NLT, NKJV.

....

Lizbeth Pioquinto is a dedicated housewife and mother from Florida. She is actively involved in her church, where she shares the Good News through street evangelism, with a focus on the local Hispanic community.

Alissia Miles

Adhere to the Stone

To the righteous whose foundation is sure but who may struggle adhering to the Stone. Greetings in the name of our Lord and Savior Jesus Christ. The purpose of my writing is to remind you that perilous times are here, and to be an effective living letter, it is essential to rest on and be supported by a solid, sure, and immovable foundation. Not only are we to be held up by an immovable foundation, but we are to be wise builders and build upon it. Jesus, the Chief Cornerstone, is our sure foundation.

A Proper Foundation

> *"Therefore thus says the Lord God, Behold, I am laying in Zion for a foundation a Stone, a tested Stone, a precious Cornerstone of sure foundation;*

> *he who believes (trusts in, relies on, and adheres to that Stone) will not be ashamed or give way or hasten away [in sudden panic]"* (Isaiah 28:16 AMPC).

The cornerstone is a crucial stone in the making of a building. It is the first piece placed in the construction to give direction in laying the foundation. Then, all the other stones are positioned about it. The foundation is the hidden piece that carries the weight of a structure and the very things that reside in it. Yes, the important hidden thing that, if we're not careful, can be forgotten about. We may not see the foundation; however, the building will show evidence of whether or not it was laid properly or neglected. The builder's work is divided into phases, and laying and framing the foundation is the longest part of the construction process. I want to dig deep into these phases to help us get an understanding of how they relate to us spiritually by coming from a natural standpoint.

Excavation

The worksite must be cleared and prepared before laying the foundation. The excavation process involves digging into the earth to remove soil, vegetation, debris, roots, and anything else that will hinder the creation of the proper space for the foundation. When an individual receives Jesus as their personal Lord and Savior and decides to let go of the things that separate them from Him, He begins a process by the Holy Spirit to move things that would hinder us. When we are willing, the Spirit of God works on us to excavate the corrupt ways and habits that we have given ourselves over to, and

He uses some of our experiences to mold and shape us to the dimensions necessary for His will for our lives.

Reinforcement

Once the space has been prepared, there are steps necessary to protect the integrity of the prepared space. In the process of reinforcement, rebars are placed inside the area to keep it from chipping and deforming as shifts occur in the soil. I would view the soil as life happening and the warfare associated with that, and the rebar as the word of God. God's word, along with His Spirit, enables us to stand on a sure foundation. By studying the word of God, we learn who Christ is and what He has done for us, which is the basis of having a foundation in Him.

As quoted above, I like how Isaiah 28:16 (AMPC) puts it: *"he who believes (trusts in, relies on, and adheres to that Stone) will not be ashamed or give way or hasten away [in sudden panic]."* In the times ahead, we must be founded upon the Rock and totally adhere to Him. According to Merriam-Webster, adhere means:

1. To hold fast or stick by or as if by gluing, suction, grasping, or fusing
2. To give support or maintain loyalty
3. To bind oneself to observance

We must hold fast to the word of God, which is a lamp unto our feet and a light unto our path. The word of God is truth. When the enemy's lies are thrown in your face, and when false doctrine arises, you will know what is true because you adhere to the word of God. It may seem so simple because we already know this, right? But if you're like me (I hope not), sometimes it just takes a minute to catch a clue. So, when the times of testing and proving show up in your life, will you hold fast? Will you be glued to the foundation you have in Christ? Will you remain loyal unto God amid chaos and deception? This is when knowing you are on a secure foundation is key because this Stone has already been tested and is sure. For this reason, you will not be caught off guard or taken aback because you have Christ as the foundation of every area of your life, and you can honestly say that you trust and rely on Him. So in chaotic situations, you will not be put to shame or be in panic. Our foundation is eternal. I'm reminded of a song lyric, "build your hopes on things eternal, hold to God's unchanging hand."

> *"So everyone who hears these words of Mine and acts upon them [obeying them] will be like a sensible (prudent, practical, wise) man who built his house upon the rock. And the rain fell and the floods came and the winds blew and beat against that house; yet it did not fall, because it had been founded on the rock"* (Matthew 7:24-25 AMPC).

Concrete

The next phase of the process is concrete pouring. Acts 1:8 (NKJV) states: *"But you shall receive power when the Holy Spirit has come upon you."* This is a key part of our process:

receiving the gift of His Holy Spirit. His Spirit keeps us, teaches us, and leads us into all truth and righteousness in God. Can you visualize the concrete being poured into the space that was made from the excavation process? This process leaves no room for anything else to occupy the area. Matthew 12:43-45 (NKJV) states: *"When an unclean spirit goes out of a man, he goes through dry places, seeking rest, and finds none. Then he says, 'I will return to my house from which I came.' And when he comes, he finds it empty, swept, and put in order. Then he goes and takes with him seven other spirits more wicked than himself, and they enter and dwell there; and the last state of that man is worse than the first."* When we have gone through the excavation and reinforcement process, the space needs to be filled with the Holy Spirit. As we spend time in prayer and water ourselves through the word of God, we can then go through a curing period that strengthens our relationship with God and makes us more sensitive to the leading of His Spirit.

Curing

Curing is the final stage of laying a foundation. This is the start of the hydration process, when water is added to the cement, causing a reaction to form a strong bond. To maintain moisture, one of these methods is used: 1) wet curing, which involves curing blankets being placed on the surface to keep it wet for a number of days, 2) fogging, which keeps the concrete wet by placing a mist above it to slow evaporation and shrinkage, or 3) ponding, which is the process of creating a pool of water around the concrete. Just like the concrete has to be strong, we as a body of believers need to be strong as well. It is important to be covered and supported and to build strong bonds within a church community. Surrounding ourselves with like-minded people will position us to be sharpened instead of shrinking and becoming dry.

A Wise Builder

As a living letter, what we do and don't do will affect the world around us. While being carried and held up by a firm foundation, we are to build upon it. Since the foundation has been laid, we must be careful how we build upon it, for we are God's building, according to 1 Corinthians 3:9-15. That means in whatever we try to build, not only does it have to have value but eternal value. It also means doing what we were called and graced to do and reaching those around us. My husband used a demonstration of the game Jenga in a message he preached. He talked about how experiences and disappointments in life are to get us to know the character of God and for foundation building. However, when we have the wrong perspective concerning those experiences because it doesn't feel good or we've become disappointed in certain areas, we begin to disregard those lessons and want to pull them out from our foundation instead of allowing them to develop our relationship with God and know His character.

This makes the foundation unstable, and after a while, if we continue to pull the pieces out, Jenga! Our world comes crashing down! When we change our perspective about our experiences and learn from them, we can use this as a testimony for others who may need to hear it, which is also a part of building.

Effects of a Faulty Foundation

If there are no regular foundation inspections, telltale signs of a faulty foundation will begin to show up. Do you know the signs of when a foundation needs to be repaired? When the home moves from its intended or original elevation, it is then time for foundation repair. You will notice the home moving in a downward or sinking manner. The movement isn't noticeable all at once, but the shifting happens gradually over time, which is why foundation issues are likely ignored. The problem arises when swelling soils occur along with weather conditions going from extremely wet to dry year after year.

The signs of a foundation problem are many, but I'll touch on a few. One of the first signs will be diagonal cracks in the walls and stair-step cracks in the bricks. Another sign is doors that stick, making it difficult to close and open them properly. Gaps can occur around windows and cabinetry that causes separation from the walls.

Foundation Inspection

In most cases, common home issues can be traced back to the foundation underneath the surface. This can be that the foundation itself is causing issues or that problems like expansive soils or weather conditions are affecting the foundation. When it comes to us, this can look like we've built our lives on another foundation. You know, those things that we place above and in the place of God (idols), such as power, self, money, people, and the list can go on and on. Then there are the expansive soils and weather conditions that are like the fiery trials that 1 Peter 4:12 mentions.

It is important for homeowners to be aware of their home so they know when an inspector is needed. Access must be granted for an inspector to take a thorough look at the interior and exterior of the home. The inspector's goal is to determine the structural integrity of the home and if the foundation is properly up to code. The Holy Spirit is our inspector, and I believe that we should allow Him regular access to check if we are properly up to code and maintaining the intended elevation. Being up to code is aligning with His statutes, His truths, and His will for our lives.

Over the last year, the Lord has been getting my attention to focus on foundation and establishing order within my home. I can honestly say that throughout last year, my family's gaze had shifted, and the Lord was letting me know that we needed to come back to code. We had to come back to the point where we were truly grounded in Him and keep Him at the center of everything we do.

My Personal Experience

I am a witness to the outcome of a neglected faulty foundation. Some time ago, we noticed small cracks forming in the walls of the house we were renting. We made sure to take pictures right away and sent them to the property manager so the landlord would be aware of the issue. Within a two-year timeframe, what started as small cracks turned into many long cracks from windows to the middle of the walls. The floors that were once levelled had become unlevelled. The concrete floors were cracked and lifted underneath the carpet of the living room. It looked like a hot mess on the inside, and not only that, you could also tell there were foundation issues from the outside. As we saw how things were worsening, we kept sending pictures to the landlord, but it wasn't a pressing matter to them. Finally, when the home got to its ugliest state, and there was no denying that we had a problem, the landlord sent an inspector to evaluate the damages.

During that time, we were facing foundational issues with the house we were living in, but the people living in the house were having spiritual foundational issues, and the telltale signs were cracks in the room of our hearts. It was like the very house I saw falling apart before my eyes was a reflection of what was going on within my family. We had gone through several experiences, problem after problem, and somewhere down the line, our hearts were in delicate places.

Bitterness, anger, rejection, pride, unforgiveness, fear, anxiety, insecurity, isolation, grief, trauma, resentment, and unhealed wounds were coming up to the surface. Why? Because of the hidden things that were never inspected and which over time spilled out and were now a mess. The appearance of our home got to the point where it was no longer attractive on the inside. We were embarrassed to invite anyone over because it was not appealing. Also, when it came to the cracks of my heart, I wasn't letting anybody in because it was straight jacked up. The storms of life hit and hit hard, so that somewhere down the line, my foundation was shaken and sinking. Yes, I was a believer in Jesus Christ and loved him with my heart (so I thought); however, being truly devoted to Him in the midst of chaotic situations was questionable. Yes, I carried the Bible and read it from time to time, but did I adhere to the words and live them out? Absolutely not! My house was sinking while my faith was being tested.

The rains came and flooded all around me. The winds came and blew up in my face. There were gaps in my walls due to the shaken foundation. What do you do in this state? I realized it was time for an inspection and repair. I had to go back to the basics of my foundation, learn Jesus all over again, and fix my gaze upon him to remain connected. I had to let Him dig deep in those sensitive areas of my heart and uproot and clear the debris that had kept me at a distance and hindered me from truly embracing who I am in God and the call He has placed on my life. When in this position, it blocks you from functioning at full capacity and stops you from building and utilizing your giftings to serve others well. I was serving; however, what I was saying as a living letter was that I was damaged, unstable, and leaky.

We do not want our lives to be read in that manner but rather to be read as strengthened, secure, and stable in the One whom we say we serve. I'm reminded of a message Apostle Raine preached, where she was talking about being built up in strong devotion, which means "to demonstrate a love for God that is undeniable, a loyalty to Him that cannot be persuaded otherwise, and an enthusiasm for our God and His works in the earth and His plan." We are to love the Lord our God, walk in His ways, and serve Him with our whole hearts while keeping His commandments and statutes (Deuteronomy 10:12-13).

I want to love God where there is no denying it and be loyal to Him in the midst of trials. While in the process of testing, I want everything that is not like God to be removed and everything that is of value and eternal to remain, and I want the same for you! Regular foundation inspections should be an ongoing thing for us. When our gaze is upon Jesus, we don't have to worry about losing our intended elevation in Him or falling away. In these perilous times that are here and to come, we are going to have to keep our eyes on Him. We will see things we have never seen before or didn't even think we would experience, but I am here to remind you to stand firm in the Lord and in the power of His might. Stay girded! Stay praying! Stay fasting! Adhere to the Stone!

Alissia Miles

References

Hearns, Alicia. "Compressive Strength of Concrete: The Best Curing Techniques." *Giatec Scientific Inc.*, https://www.giatecscientific.com/education/curing-techniques-for-measuring-the-compressive-strength-of-concrete/. Accessed 23 January, 2025.

"How Does Concrete Cure?" *Marstellar Oil and Concrete*, 8 August, 2018, https://marstellaroilconcrete.com/blog/how-does-concrete-cure/. Accessed 22 January, 2025.

Lewis, Austin. "What Even Is Foundation Repair and How Is It Done?" *Anchor Foundation Repair*, 16 November, 2023, https://anchorfoundationrepair.net/blog/what-how-foundation-repair-done/. Accessed January 2025.

....

Alissia Miles is a wife, mother, psalmist, and author of *The Heat, the Hustle, & the Drive (Life from a Basketball Mom's Perspective)*. She enjoys creating things with her hands, spending time with her family, and relaxing. Alissia resides in Dallas, Texas, with her husband, Tyshawn, and their four amazing children.

Lisa Michelle Beeler

Family – Fitting the Fruits Together

The Head Man

Having a biological father and a stepfather growing up was my biggest life-changing experience. The former was a strong man that was a protector and a provider with the emotional flaw of being stressed by his commitment to his job and extended family. He went to church and later became an associate pastor. A heavy weight to carry, leading him to take his own life.

The latter was a strategic man that was a provider and life-changer. He struggled with his manhood and was influenced by women and organizations. He had a testimony of getting his master's in theology and said his purpose was to minister to his family. He knew his diagnosis was COPD and would love his blended family with his last breath.

The root of motherhood: knowing that God had allowed her to hold a seed and breathed His very breath into my dust to create a living and breathing being. I was formed in my mother's womb.

She had a plan to be in a covenant with a man as a wife, and she nurtured and cared for me in her daily life. During my age of awareness as a teenager, her reassurance and our time together went to a different stage, as I became independent as a young adult. *"When I was a child, I spoke as a child ... but when I became a man, I put away childish things"* (1 Corinthians 13:11 NKJV).

Forbearance

The world and things are no longer familiar. The innocence of a child is very precious. Every child and person has left, but I am pointing in a vertical direction to God. Who is at the core is my God and me. As a nine-year-old, I felt the guilt of silence with molestation from a close cousin, not knowing I would have to forgive and confront the same person as an adult without a request to forgive or repentance in return.

Taking the life of a child is meaningless. As I turned 13 years old, I remember getting the news from my mother and seeing it on the local news that my four-year-old cousin had been beaten to death by my aunt's boyfriend. I was beating the wall with my fist in rage. That caused me to be apprehensive of love and appreciate the love I have now.

I came home from singing in the Capital University Gospel Choir as a college student. God spoke to me, and I was praying and shouting in my parents' dining room. "God, You said I was going to be married, and You said I was going to have kids!" I was worshipping and praising God in the Holy Ghost. My father tried to calm me down, and my mother was weeping. God got the glory with his witnesses worshipping in agreement on my behalf. *"Look now toward heaven, and tell the stars ... so shall thy seed be"* (Genesis 15:5 BRG). *"So from one man, though he was [physically] as good as dead, were born as many descendants as the stars of heaven in number, and innumerable as the sand on the seashore"* (Hebrews 11:12 AMP). Also see Genesis 15:5-6; 22:17; 32:12.

Love

I know that God is the center of my life, and He saved me right before I went off to college. In the summer I finished high school, I gave my life over to Christ. I believe God prepared me to go to college in Columbus, Ohio.

I dated several men in college and felt that my goal at some stage of life after graduating from college was to start my own family. I was a person who believed that being in love with the person and knowing that I wanted to marry them was the priority in any future relationship. I made the decision to let a young man into my heart who became a friend and was someone I grew into loving as a partner. Later, I was having premarital sex and being convicted every time it happened. I was an out-of-state student and ready to receive my degree as a graduate of a university that challenged me from start to finish. *"I have told you these things, so that in me you may have peace. In this world you will have trouble. But take heart! I have overcome the world"* (John 16:33 NIV).

Self-Control

A few years after I made the decision to become intimate with him, I became pregnant. The decision I made would impact my life forever. I made the decision to have an abortion and continue with graduating college. I cried out to God and asked Him to forgive me. As time went on, we were off and on for several months. I had male friends in my life, but none like this one. He would stand out to me like a sure thing that wasn't quite developed into what God had called him to be. The faith that God had given me to see in him was dwindling.

About a year later, I was preparing for graduation and became pregnant again. I was in my last semester of school when I found out that I was pregnant for the second time by the same man. This time, I didn't want to make the same mistake I had in the past. This time, I knew that the sin was committed, but a child is a blessing. I had already lost one child through abortion and wanted a serious relationship to commit to for a lifetime. Before graduation day, I had to explain to my family that I was expecting a child. We had a family meeting and discussed the importance of raising a child with both parents.

During and after giving birth, I planned the perfect life for my new family and our child. My Bible cover had the scripture, *"For I know the plans that I have towards you, plans to prosper you and not to harm you, plans to give you hope and a future"* (Jeremiah 29:11 NIV). I would sacrifice getting a dental degree to become a mother and raise my baby in a family. Of course, things didn't work out as planned.

I received a notice from my professor saying that I still had to complete three credit hours and would not be graduating on time. My heart dropped to my stomach. Not only was I pregnant, but I was also afraid that I would not finish in two months as expected. But God dispatched one of His own Angels, saying, "Write a note to the dean and tell her how the teacher miscalculated and miscued your credit hours." I did that and stayed on my knees and prayed. I later met with the dean and received a letter saying that I would graduate on time. I was able to walk down the aisle with my firstborn growing inside of me. God allowed me to have a birth that lasted only three hours. I came out of that situation into another. I tried to work things out my way in my relationship, and God said, "Not yet." At some point while we were apart, my boyfriend told me that he went to church, gave his life to Christ, and was saved.

The journey hit another stumbling block. There was a time in my life when I decided to move out in rebellion and was homeless. Not only was I working a job as a dental assistant and going to school but also taking care of a child that was innocent as they come. We found ourselves homeless with nowhere to lay our heads. We later found shelter on a blanket in a vacant house for rent. I said, "I can't go back home," but God told me to come home. And so, I did. I was living in an abandoned house with my baby, sleeping on the floor with her car seat. I was an independent single mother; I talked to my boss and told him my situation, and he said, "It's time to go home." I used my paycheck and packed all my things in a car and went home. I went to my parents' house and spoke to my mother, only to be rejected and told that I would have to pay rent.

Kindness

I went to my grandmother's house and explained the situation to her, and she accepted me with open arms. *"So he got up and went to his father. But while he was still a long way off, his father saw him and was filled with compassion for him: he ran to his son, threw his arms around him and kissed him"* (Luke 15:20 NIV). I told her it would only be for a few months. I could pay her once I got a job and if she could watch my daughter while I found a babysitter or day care. My grandmother was the person that I spent time with every weekend before I went to college. She was going through stage four colon cancer and did not tell anyone how severe her condition was until her health was degrading.

Gentleness

My grandmother gave me exactly the strength I needed to move through this transition of my life. I assisted and cared for her with daily tasks, and she loved me unconditionally. I had a conversation with her about needing assistance and moved out to my own apartment and bought a car within two months. She said, "I'll be okay." I visited her every day until the last day, when she said, "I want to go to church." I got her wheelchair out and took her. I looked over and she began to get sick in church. I began to roll her out, and the pastor stopped his sermon and prayed for her. She went to the hospital and later went into hospice care to transition to heaven. I lost my best friend and would remember the matriarch, spiritual leader of the church, and female legacy that I was left behind to model.

Raising a Family – Faithfulness

Shortly after, the person that impacted my life expressed his feelings for me and confessed to having a baby on the way. He told me that he wanted to be with me and marry me after all. I packed up my belongings and moved back to Ohio, where we were married a few months later and started to add to our family immediately. My husband and I were married, and I never would have made it without God. Time passed as a blended family of two; there were now three, and soon to be four children to raise in a household, as God had intended with all the twists and turns of life. After having houses that went into foreclosure and purchasing a new house, we had to live in different states and have a long-distance relationship. Now, after 20 years married, we are in a position that puts a bind in the structure of the family. In the best and the worst of times, I will allow God to mend broken hearts.

Positive Spirit – Goodness

The ministry of dance is doing a service for the Lord through movement and giving Him all He deserves with our whole hearts, minds, bodies, and souls. I was introduced to dancing in church at the very young age of three. This is one of the reasons I minister in dance in college. In 2007, I accepted the appointment into the dance ministry because I love the feeling I get when I minister in dance. I get this overwhelming sense of comfort. I notice that while I am ministering that it's not me at all, it's the Holy Spirit within me. I focus a large amount of time and energy into the technique of dance. I minister in dance because it gives me joy, and I feel like I get rid of all the burdens and baggage that I have harbored for so long. It's truly my release for all the frustration and strongholds I have bound, and He gives me freedom to worship. I am going through spiritual warfare and prayer intercession for those who are not strong enough to fight and are bound. *"For the weapons of our warfare are not carnal, but mighty through God to the pulling down of strongholds"* (2 Corinthians 10:4 KJ21).

The day that I knew that God was working on my behalf was when my home church gave me the Positive Spirit Award for 2024. Over the years, He has allowed me to break out of the box, evangelize, dance, and meet people from all over the world. What a wonderful thing to see His destiny unfold!

Peace

I am dealing with being a caregiver to my mother, who was diagnosed with Alzheimer's and dementia symptoms. As dementia has developed in my mother, the focus of care needed is promoting passive involvement and some level of comfort, caring, and contentment. One of the questions raised is, can you get out of the bed? A person functioning at a healthy cognitive level can get the family out of the door.

My mental health is purified every day by spending time with God, His Word, and devotion. *"Create in me a clean heart, O God; and renew a right spirit within me"* (Psalms 51:10 KJV). My motto is and will always be, "Die Daily." To live for Jesus Christ, Lisa has to die daily.

Fruitfulness Is the Goal

Now I ask the question: What type of fruit are you producing in character? I have been an ordained minister for 10 years and in leadership as a minister of dance for 20 years in multiple states, equipping youth and adults across the region. I know that using my gifts and seeing the fruit through children and youth growing into adults is a reward for God. As I get older, I ask myself the questions: Can I survive for nine months without electricity? Can I grow my own garden? My goal is opening my own fruit and vegetable garden and being self-sufficient in my new home. What kind of fruit are you producing in spirit? *"But the fruit of the spirit is love, joy peace, forbearance, kindness, goodness, faithfulness, gentleness and self-control. Against such things there is no law"* (Galatians 5:22-23 NIV).

Lisa Michelle Beeler

Lisa Michelle Beeler was introduced to the gifts of dance and vocal music at a young age. She participated in Young Author's Award and Youth Gospel Workshops, and is saved through Jesus. She holds a bachelor's in biology and an MBA, and she is a licensed Minister. She is mother to Zion, Aakilah, David, and Yamani.

www.ingramcontent.com/pod-product-compliance
Lightning Source LLC
LaVergne TN
LVHW020048110826
845155LV00029B/682